SHE IS STRO

II

The

GREAT CANADIAN
Woman

For permission requests, write to
The Great Canadian Woman at:
team@thegreatcanadianwoman.ca

Published by The Great Canadian Woman Publishing
www.thegreatcanadianwoman.ca

Quantity sales. Special discounts are available on quantity purchases by corporations, associations, and others.
For details, contact The Great Canadian
Woman head office at the address above.

ISBN 978-1-9992151-1-8

Cover Designed by Falon Malec
Book Designed by Doris Chung
Edited by Christine Stock

SHE IS STRONG AND FREE II

The
GREAT CANADIAN
Woman

JACKIE VANDERLINDEN

CINDY GOCH, LINDSAY ANDERSON, ERIN MONTGOMERY, PEGGY BIRR,
LISA DI DOMENICO, MARNY WILLIAMS-BALODIS, JANICE GLADUE, LIZ PRACSOVICS,
KIMBERLY DAVIS, JESSICA DANFORD, EMILY MURCAR, JANE MIDDLEHURST,
TRISHA DOHARTY, AMANDA STEWART, SARAH VAILL-CIANO, KOA BAKER,
REBEKAH JANE MERSEREAU

Contents

One of These Things Is Not Like the Others . . . 3

Mental Illness and Parenting Can Co-Exist 21

Connection Through Great Things 37

Love, Marriage, Empty Carriage 53

Social Work Burnout to Spiritual Breakout 71

From Child to Certified to Coach 95

The Good, the Bad, and the Unfaithful 113

Perseverance, Kindness, and Becoming a Goddamn Warrior 127

Taking Back My Life 145

Birth and Rebirth 167

Breaking the Silence 191

Esmerelda and the Golden Nuggets 207

Rising through the Dark Night of the Soul 223

Breakthrough 247

My Unbecoming 269

My Pursuit to Fulfilment 285

I Am a Lighthouse 307

My Blessing and My Curse 325

Author Bios

Janice Gladue	16
Koa Baker	33
Rebekah Jane Mersereau	49
Amanda Stewart	66
Lindsay Anderson	91
Emily Murcar	109
Erin Montgomery	123
Sarah Vaill-Ciano	140
Jessica Danford	163
Cindy Goch	187
Liz Pracsovics	203
Marny Williams-Balodis	218
Kimberly Davis	243
Trisha Doharty	265
Lisa Di Domenico	281
Peggy Birr	302
Jane Middlehurst	320
Jackie VanderLinden	336

INTRODUCTION

Welcome! We are so honoured you are here. Before you dive in, it's important to know that what you have in your hands here is so much more than a book. This book holds within it the sacred lives and journeys of eighteen everyday great Canadian womxn. Sharing your story in a book means you never really know who is going to read it. This reality can create fear and hesitation for the authors. Sharing your story alongside so many others can bring up feelings of doubt and leave you wondering whether anyone will care about yours. Writing your story at all can leave you wondering if it's even worth sharing and questioning if it would even make an impact on another person's life. The eighteen womxn in this book have overcome these doubts and more, and now their stories rest within the pages of this book for you and so many others to read. These pages are filled with such emotion, rawness, hope, and heartfelt wisdom. And while words can never truly do justice to the pain and strength each story holds, we commend these womxn for their bravery in showing up for themselves and for their vulnerability.

The more we share these stories, the more walls we break down.

The more we share our darkest times, the more light we can allow in.

The more we share our truths, the more we can live authentically.

The more we share ourselves, the more we connect, uplift, and grow.

We hope that as you read these stories, you find a piece of yourself in these pages. You may find yourself relating to an experience or to an emotional process. Either way, you'll feel connected.

Thank you for supporting these authors by reading their stories.

If you have a story you would like to share in an upcoming volume, please visit www.thegreatcanadianwoman.ca for details.

Please note that these stories are real and raw and contain discussions of death, loss, grief, mental illness, suicide, addiction, and use adult language.

She Is

——— Strong

ONE OF THESE THINGS IS NOT LIKE THE OTHERS . . .

Janice Gladue

> *"Belonging is belonging to yourself first; speaking your truth, telling your story, and never betraying yourself for other people. True belonging does not require you to change who you are. It requires you to be who you are— and that's vulnerable."*
>
> *- Brené Brown, The Call to Courage*

Sometimes my mind wanders into interesting spaces. I've spent countless hours amusing myself with creative questions and ponderings. One of the recurring thoughts that I have considered is *If my life had a theme song, what would it be?* For many years, the only song that I could ever arrive at to answer this question was a song performed during a segment on *Sesame Street* called "One of These Things Is Not Like the Others."

I was a child known for having a beaming smile and possessing a generally good nature. As I grew up, I became known for being a hard worker, an excellent student, a great friend and supporter of others, and well skilled at most things I set my mind to do. I believe that most people who knew me as a child and into my years as a young adult would not have considered me a misfit, a loner, or troubled. The truth is that I was deeply troubled, and I felt like a very big misfit. And while I wasn't alone, the reality is that I felt desperately alone. At the core of my being, my truth was that I didn't belong.

I was apprehended by Social Services when I was about four years old. The sudden and quick removal of me from my family felt like a violent severing of connection and belonging, yanked full force from the ground by the roots. In one fell swoop I was tossed and plunged into a sea of uncertainty, instability, disconnection, fear, confusion, and despair. All the natural, organic parts that rooted me in life were washed away.

As I moved through the deep, cold, stormy waters, I struggled incessantly with finding my bearings. No matter the extent of the effort I committed, I couldn't quite get a grasp of where I was or truly know my place. As a little girl, I ached for love and affection. I craved reassurance, but I was denied it. I fought to find my footing, to find even just a sliver of solid ground. There was nobody to hold me while I cried myself to sleep, nobody interested in witnessing my pain, no one to wipe my tears. Bedtime hugs were forbidden and general chatter and inquisitive conversation by children discouraged. Looking back, I can see that I was stranded in this unforgiving and unrelenting sea for so long—left to sink or swim.

The details that led to my apprehension do not reside in my memory and have only been populated by sparse stories and memories shared by others. The parts of my early life story that I don't need others to fill in for me are of all the pain and desperation I experienced and not knowing where I belonged or to whom I belonged. Even now, as I sit to put it into words, my body remembers the trauma—revisiting it all is an authentic and present experience.

I was apprehended and placed into care along with the youngest of my five brothers. I don't remember much specifically about our first foster home, but what I do remember vividly is that my brother, two years my senior, was seemingly always in trouble. I was preschool-aged, and it became my regular responsibility to bring his dinner to his bedroom. There was no childish chatter, no play—only the business of bringing him food and retrieving his dirty dinnerware after. His bedroom was where he was sentenced to serve his punishment for the crime of being an Indian. It is so strange that at such a young age I recognized that. He was always in trouble for things that occurred at school. He was never heard;

his side of any story didn't matter. His condemnation was predetermined. At each instance, our foster parent clearly stated that *it was her job to raise us to be good Indian children*. At four years old, I didn't understand with full reason and words what this meant or the weight it carried, but my heart felt it with immense effect.

The next home we moved to was very different. The farmland was vast with barns that housed animals I had never seen up close and personal in my life. There were dogs, cats, cows, and pigs. There were no other homes to be seen on the horizon. I had nothing familiar to grasp onto besides my brother. He was unsteady and out of sorts, just as I was. This situation is where my temporary situation became a permanent condition, or so it seemed.

Nobody fought for me. Nobody came to get me. Nobody came to see if I was okay. Nobody visited. Nobody showed me affection. Nobody cared.

Nobody loved me.

* * *

When you are a child, it is hard to make sense of all the things that are happening around you. For me, this was only exacerbated by the circumstance of my life. Everything, and I mean *everything*, was foreign to me—the people, the language, the culture, the lifestyle, the land. There was no reprieve from stress and confusion. There was a constant requirement for me to try to make sense of foreign, strange, and often traumatic experiences. I was always unsure of what was real or stable.

I soon developed some survival mechanisms to manage the mess. I moved through childhood, fulfilling the role expected of me (to be a cute, polite, well-behaved, hard-working, and high-achieving child), pretending and strategically adapting as each situation required. Over time I put up façades, armoured up, barricaded my heart, learned how to navigate relationships (always sure not to go too deep), and developed grit and resolve inside while being bright and agreeable outside. There was such a duality, and sometimes multiplicity, to my being that there is no wonder that I had such a struggle with belonging. I could not reconcile who I was in the world, let alone to myself.

My childhood was multi-faceted and complicated. It isn't my intention to make light of what I experienced, it's just that it tends to get convoluted and messy to share a full, collective experience. So, I find the stories and events are much easier to tell as singular moments. Lots of things happened in my life, some tougher than others, and some joyful. However, when I was a kid, while "things were happening," I also endured repeated sexual abuse. It started when I was about five years old. Every morning, day after day, one of the biological sons of my foster parents would quietly come to my bedside after he made his lunch for work. I pretended to be asleep while I screamed in anguish inside. I didn't tell anyone about it until I was nineteen years old. For so many years, I put on a smile and played a role. I never was any trouble, and I was obedient and high achieving.

I lived in this foster home for thirteen years. For some, the length of time in one place would be regarded as a win, but despite the years there, I never belonged. I worked hard to be the kind of kid they wanted (whatever that meant). Over time I grew to accept them as my parents and to love them, mostly out of necessity as a human being. However, like with most things, it was an arrangement. There were rules, which meant any love came with rules and boundaries—it was not free and full. Their love was always conditional. I can vividly recall so many instances and experiences when I was clearly shown that I didn't belong. There were so many times when conditions for their love were stated, and I was reminded that my situation was precarious. Subtlety was not a trait of my foster family in this regard.

My foster family was Mennonite, and Low German was spoken frequently in the home. To the foster children (sometimes there were up to three or four others in addition to my brother and me), Low German was like a secret language they used to keep us kids from knowing what was going on. It wasn't done out of kindness to spare innocent children exposure to painful details. It was indeed about keeping us in the dark.

We went to church *a lot*. When I was little, we usually attended twice on Sunday and at least once during the week for bible study. In my teen years, I attended church and church functions up to a total of five times a week. The church was a big deal in our household. When we first began attending church, my foster family would regularly discuss my situation with others in front of me, making me feel embarrassed and small. As time passed, they began to introduce me as their "foster daughter," always clear to emphasize the distinction. My foster mom sewed me pretty church dresses. I was very proud and felt very special in them. But then, to keep my ego in check, they would give me the ugliest, old-man shoes to wear with them. The stifling of my joy was a regular occurrence.

Once, we went for family pictures. My foster parents, their biological children, and my brother and I got dressed in our Sunday best. It was pretty exciting. I had never been to a studio before, so it was an extraordinary experience for me. The photographer positioned us all together and made adjustments as he snapped photo after photo. And then, when the photographer asked my foster parents if there were any other photos they would like, they responded, "Yes, we'd like some with *just the family* now." My brother and I were removed from the group. And even as my heart broke, I resolved not to give them the satisfaction of seeing it.

Visits with my biological family were always bittersweet happenings. There was so much anticipation and excitement in the days and hours leading up to seeing them. The truth is that times with my family were not all celebrations. They were awkward and cumbersome as we all tried to reconcile the immense joy of being together with the hurt and anguish of all the experiences that kept us apart. Everyone worked hard to temper sadness and dared not speak of reality for fear that it would overshadow the small, fleeting opportunity to exchange and experience love. As time passed and things got more complicated, the connectedness and belonging to my root family weakened.

After visits with my family, I would return to my foster home and to church where I was told in no uncertain terms that the spiritual practices of my family and community were pagan and "of the devil." It was as if I was never allowed to hold anything sacred and special in my life; I had nothing to love and hold dear. Nothing was safe from being tainted by the judgment and expectations of others.

I experienced bedwetting until I was about twelve years old. When I was in grade 3, my foster parents got me a vibrating mesh-screen bedwetting alarm pad that went under my bedsheets. It was uncomfortable on many levels, and the alarm was jarring and just plain horrible. It would go off, and I would wake up in an absolute panic, not only about the need to clean up my bed but more so because I knew that I would have to contend with a heap of trouble. Whenever I wet the bed, I was not only made to feel bad about myself and what I had done but I also had to wash my wet bedclothes, underwear, and sheets in a pail by hand. Shaming was a major thing in our household. In each instance, I would cry, my hands in a bucket full of water, and I would have to sit in the middle of the house (not discreetly tucked into a quiet corner) and be made to pose for a photo.

My foster parents' extended family was quite large. On Sunday afternoons between morning church and evening service we would go to a gathering of aunts, uncles, cousins, and family friends. Most of the get-togethers happened at someone's farm. The kids would run around the large yard, playing until being called for *faspa* (a light meal). When *faspa* was ready, the other parents called their children by their names. Mine called me "Piddles" (you know, an affectionate nickname to recognize that I was a proficient bed-wetter). I'm sure you can guess how all the kids responded to that one. Once again, I was utterly devastated, but of course, like many things, I just had to grin and bear it.

Each year for my birthday, my foster mom made a delicious homemade cake heaped with sweet buttercream frosting. After dinner, the cake would be brought out, candles flickering brightly, while everyone sang "Happy Birthday." I felt very special and loved by all the extra effort and attention that marked my birthday. Ooh, and what child doesn't like gifts? I would excitedly tear at the beautiful wrapping paper. And as the contents of the package were revealed, I would fight back tears and grin the best I could. The happiness and exhilaration of the moment were quickly destroyed by being made to "proudly" show off gifts of diapers, toddler panties, and baby toys while being called names, laughed at, and shamed in countless other ways.

When I was about fourteen years old, I was standing in the kitchen with my foster mom when she took a call from Social

Services. I could hear just enough of what the caller was saying to make sense of the discussion. The discussion was to advise my foster mom that there was a new training requirement for all foster parents. My foster mom bluntly stated that she and her husband had been foster parents for many years and that she was confident that they knew how to do the job. The person from Social Services indicated that if they did not get the training, they would not get paid for my care, to which my foster mom responded (without hesitation before abruptly hanging up the phone), "Come get her then." There must have been more discussions that occurred after that because Social Services never did come and get me. And I do recall hearing that a deal was struck that they would not be required to take the new training but that I would be the only and last foster child who would be allowed in their care. I remember questioning how, after so many years, they could be so willing to cast me aside so quickly over a dispute about money. It was then that I realized my place in the family was bought and paid for in instalments; I was purely a business transaction.

Things began to unravel when I was in high school, and it was not because I was a handful or a bad kid. I was quite the opposite. But for some reason things took a strange turn, and my foster parents stopped talking to me, not a little bit but all together, for days. My foster mother even went so far as to put a piece of duct tape over her mouth for a brief time. All these years later, I still can't put my finger on the reason why.

I struggled for a long time to come up with a solution to the situation at home. Ultimately, I ended up using the school phone to call my social worker. I don't recall if I had to look it up or if I knew the number. After all, for years it was common practice for my foster parents to give me the number after each time I got the strap so that I could *tell on them* if I wanted to. I digress. My social worker, Nancy, decided that she would arrange to come for a lunch meeting with my foster parents. It was an awkward lunch. Not much was said, but when words were spoken, they packed a punch.

The silence and tension were thick. Nancy attempted to encourage a conversation to sort out what the problem was. Suddenly, just a few minutes into lunch and with plates still full of food, my foster dad stood up, stepped back from the table and said without hesitation, "If you are thinking about moving, you move today. What you don't take with you today is ours to sell." Gawd! I was seventeen! I had lived with them for thirteen years, and this?! This is what it all amounted to?! In one grand flourish I was cast away, homeless, and unwanted. I belonged to no one. I belonged nowhere.

These are just some of the tough things I endured, a sort of "Coles Notes" if you will. I share them to illustrate and punctuate that the challenges I experienced with belonging were multi-faceted, enduring, traumatic, and complicated. My journey as a young girl into adulthood was all this and so much more.

I am now in my forties, a proud mother of two girls, living a full and happy life with my partner who is a fantastic father and an amazing human being. I have a fulfilling career and am blessed in many ways. I look back on my early childhood and coming into adulthood with compassion for my younger self. I recall days and nights filled with deep, dark, endless despair and gut-wrenching, heaving cries that gave no relief to my situation or condition. There were periods of never-ending darkness and unshakable heaviness. I fought desperately to find relief from the pain with little reprieve. I was perpetually alone, longing to belong. Today, I am amazed by the strength, resilience, and courage I was able to summon somehow. I recognize the guidance and protection of my ancestors and the uplifting support of many earth angels, for which I am eternally grateful.

For so many years, fear and shame ruled how I navigated life. I always felt troubled and like a misfit and a loner. I didn't just hide who I was from others, I also hid from myself. I worked hard not to be a failure, to prove everybody who expected so little of me wrong. There were so many barriers and obstacles. Sometimes it just felt like I couldn't catch a break. No matter what I did or achieved, it never felt like enough. I never felt like *I* was ever enough. I have learned to look back on my experiences and connect with my past self with compassion and grace. I can better understand the disconnection, mistrust, and the deep, strong roots of fear and shame I grappled with then and, to some degree, still have to contend with now. For many years, I rigorously stifled my voice and my joy, hiding the essence of who I am from others. It is only in recent times that I have begun to turn my collective experiences, my journey, upside down, forward and backward to gain different perspectives. I have committed immense time and effort on my own and with the help of therapists, counsellors, clinical psychologists, and several personal- and professional-development practitioners to reframe these childhood experiences in a new, healthier way for myself as an adult. Healing and growing is a messy, exhausting business, but it is well worth it all.

After all the struggle, all the hard, gritty, dirty work of fighting people, places, the elements, time, the system, etc., I think I am finding my way. And while I still have episodes where the theme song "One of These Things Is Not Like the Others" begins to play, it doesn't have the same impact anymore. It's time for a new theme song—something uplifting, bright, joyful, and inspiring, perhaps.

We can get a great, new, empowering theme song, change the storylines, reassign roles, and even make ourselves the star. We are the designers, the writers, the orators, the crafters, and the producers of the stories of our lives. We need to decide what role we are going to play on the production team.

Janice Gladue

Upon meeting Janice Gladue, you will quickly notice her bright smile, engaging personality, and relaxed conversation. To meet her today, one would not likely consider Janice to have come through much hardship in life. Truth be told, she has faced many adversities in life, including those she suffered due to her experiences in the Sixties Scoop.

Janice is an Indigenous (Cree) woman, a professional, a mother, a leader, a listener, a confidant, and a bridge builder. Her traditional name is Asini waciy iskwêw, which means Rocky Mountain Woman. Whether personal or professional, Janice works hard to foster under-standing and build capacity and connections between others. She is motivated to positively impact whatever relationship or initiative in which she might be involved. She is known to be slow to judge others and to have a voice of reason and a positive perspective to even the most trying situations.

To my beautiful girls, Xachinaa and Daniella: Your joy, curiosity, tenacity, and generosity of spirit have been healing medicine for which I am infinitely blessed and proud. You inspire me to press on, elevate, and rise above life's obstacles daily. You have shown me that true love and abundant joy are attainable and can be lasting. You are the fuel to my legacy.

She Is

Free

CHAPTER 2

MENTAL ILLNESS AND PARENTING CAN CO-EXIST

Koa Baker

I can tell you right now that I have struggled with even wanting to write about the part of my life when I struggled the most with my mental illness. Every time I have had a chance to sit and write this story for you, my dread has sunk in. Sharing my past instabilities is really scary. I feel shame and embarrassment, but I am certain that I am not the only one who has gone through something similar, and my hope is to inspire someone who is suffering to take the leap into their own healing journey and successfully manage their own mental illness.

My mental health journey has been long and hard. I have dealt with depression, anxiety, post-traumatic stress disorder (PTSD), trauma, and my eventual diagnosis of bipolar II disorder. Talking about it is hard. Writing about it is hard. Admitting how bad it got is really hard, because I never really thought that my mental health would impact my ability to mother. I never thought that I would struggle so much with my own mental health that it would make an impact on my children. When I was about to become a mother, I thought that I would be okay, that I would be happy and filled with love, joy, and attachment. I thought that the innate mother's love for her children would make all the mental health issues go away. And it didn't. If anything, becoming a mother intensified my mental illness. Becoming a mother brought my darkest days to my doorstep.

The hormones. Sleepless nights. Exhaustion. Lack of support. Figuring out how to care for a new life. All of that threw me into my worst mental state. I was irritable, angry, resentful, and hopeless. I was filled with dread and resentment. I didn't want to care for a screaming, crying, clinging, confusing little life. I barely wanted to even live myself. How could I possibly care for another life when I felt so much darkness? I suffered with those feelings for months on end. I didn't want to admit my state of mind to the doctors; I was afraid of the judgment, and I felt like a terrible mother. I was afraid that my children would be taken away from me for feeling the way I did. I was afraid that my spouse at the time would leave with my children if I told anyone what thoughts and feelings I was having. I was so scared that I would be deemed "crazy" and "unwell" that I chose to suffer alone for years instead of seeking help.

Living with mental illness is hard. It feels impossible some days. And trying to parent and raise healthy, happy, well-functioning children at the same time feels like an impossibly daunting task. How was I supposed to raise children who are mentally well when I was struggling to remain mentally well on a daily basis? Because for years, I was unstable.

There were too many days that I spent sad and crying in the bathroom with little ones on the other side of the door calling "Mommy," and I couldn't open the door and bear to look at them and let them see my pain.

There were days where I spent so much time angry and screaming instead of listening and loving.

There were too many nights my children ate cereal for dinner because I couldn't bring myself to make dinner for them.

There were many days that my children were late for school. Late to be picked up. Missing their lunch. Not dressed for the weather. Sent with unsigned forms. Wearing dirty clothes. I couldn't keep up or keep track of their school life or our simple chores at home like doing their laundry.

I can't tell you the number of times that my children had to fend for themselves by watching TV or the iPad alone in their rooms because I couldn't bring myself to interact with them. I couldn't play. I couldn't smile. I couldn't laugh. I couldn't pretend.

And at night, I would put them to bed and tell them I was sorry for having a hard day, and I would cry while they slept because I knew how badly they needed more from me and I couldn't bring myself to give them anything more.

So, I would put them to bed and drink. I drank so much that I was going to the liquor store multiple times a week to refill. I couldn't cope with my pain and guilt, and so I drank while my children slept.

One day it was just too much, and I had everything ready that I needed to kill myself. I was calm and at peace with the fact that I was done. Done feeling the mental torment. Done feeling pain. Done being a terrible mother. I was ready to quiet my mind. I was ready to commit suicide because I thought that leaving this world would be easier on my kids than the torment I was putting them through. Sometimes I think it was some kind of divine intervention that stopped me from going through with it. The calmness of accepting my suicide plan turned to worry, fear, guilt. Worry for my children. Fear that they would suffer more if I left them. Guilt that I hadn't even tried to be a better mother. Instead of taking my life that day, I chose to give my kids and myself a chance at having a happy life. I chose to change.

I wish I had known there was hope for me. I wish I had asked for help. I wish I had sought treatment. I wish that I hadn't been afraid for so long. The road to a healthy mind wasn't easy. There were a lot of tears, frustration, doctors' visits, counselling sessions, psychiatric appointments, medication changes, self-care, and a hell of a lot of internal work. But I have been well for four years now, and I am finally healing myself and my children, day by day. We all get a little bit happier and healthier with every day that passes.

Over the years I have learned what I can do for myself to help manage my mental illness. I believe that we have to put in the work to be the best version of ourselves, and I have found that these next steps are critical to mental health stability.

1. TAKE CARE OF YOURSELF FIRST.

It can be very difficult to put in the time and effort for self-care when you are a mom. Usually, we are so good at putting ourselves last. We put so much love and care into our families and home, and we don't even put in the effort to do something as simple as showering every day. I used to think a shower was a luxury as a new mom, and I would only shower every couple days. I wore the same comfy outfit multiple times a week, threw my hair in the famous mom bun, and never took time away from my children. We are taught that this is what a good mom does—she invests *everything* into her family and puts herself on the back burner. But I can promise you that investing everything in your family is a really good way to burn yourself out. Self-care is a critical aspect of thriving mental health. It isn't easy to make the time for ourselves, and sometimes we don't have the support at home that we need to get away, but self-care can take many forms.

Showering, doing your hair, putting on clean clothes and maybe even a little mascara or nail polish is self-care. Eating food that makes you feel healthy, energetic, and nourished is self-care. Doing an at-home workout in the kids' playroom while they play around you (and probably jump all over you) is self-care. If you have the luxury of having a supportive spouse or family member at home, I encourage you to take time for yourself daily. Yes, daily. Whether it's thirty minutes or two hours, you need that reset each day in order to be your best self. Shower alone, meditate, have a nap, listen to music and go for a walk, head to a coffee shop, hang out with a friend—whatever makes you feel like you are refreshed is what you need to be doing for yourself every day.

My self-care routine looks something like this:

Diet: I follow a very healthy vegan diet, which I don't push on anyone, but this is the way of eating that I found has worked best for my mental health. Find a whole- and natural-foods diet that works for your body. I also take daily vitamins along with my nutritional plan. Find a nutritionist or naturopath who can help you with a plan if you don't know where to start.

Exercise: I used to do at-home workouts when my kids were young because it was the easiest way to get in the exercise. Find an online platform, wake up early, and get in a workout a few times a week. Now that my kids are older, and I have help, I am able to go to the gym and get out for hikes. Getting into nature is my favourite kind of exercise!

Sleep: I go to bed at the same time every night (9:00 p.m.), and I wake up at 6:00 a.m. I never stay up late, and I don't mess with my sleep. This schedule has been paramount in my functioning mental health.

Routine: I try to make sure that every morning I can get up and have my coffee and relax before jumping into the day, even if it means waking up a bit earlier to get those moments alone. Being able to wake up, have coffee, eat, shower, and get ready to take on the day makes a huge difference.

Small amounts of self-care go a long way. It can change your mood from a worn-out, overworked, over-tired, impatient mom to a refreshed, calm, happy mom. Not only does self-care benefit you, it benefits your kids.

2. SEEK HELP FROM FAMILY AND FRIENDS.

Why is it that we moms think we can do it all and never ask for or need help? We seem to think that we are superheroes and can do everything ourselves. I sympathize because I used to be that supermom until I hit my breaking point. Raising kids isn't meant to be done alone. Many of us are single moms and don't have that spouse at home to help. I used to be one of those single moms. But if you try, you will find wonderful people in your life willing to help. Family, friends, women you meet at moms' groups—there are people out there who are willing and able to help you. If you are struggling with your mental health, you need to ask for help; you can't do it all alone. It can be very hard to admit that you are struggling mentally. As moms, we feel like we should be filled with love and happiness, but that's not always the case at all. It is normal to feel sadness, loneliness, frustration, and overwhelm some days. What isn't normal is the expectation that we are supposed to just stuff those feelings away and push through.

Find a person who is safe and who you trust to talk to and to ask for help when you are struggling. Having someone to confide in when you are struggling can make all the difference. I bet you will be surprised at how understanding some people can be and with how much it helps having someone you can rely on, especially on your worst days.

3. SEEK HELP FROM MEDICAL PROFESSIONALS.

Having someone to rely on and confide in can make a world of a difference, but that isn't always enough. If you are doing self-care and have support and you are still struggling, you may need to seek help from a doctor. I know that seems scary. I remember the first time I saw my doctor when my babies were young. I sobbed the entire visit as I told her about how I had been feeling; how low I had sunk. But I left there feeling heard, seen, understood, and with hope that I was going to get better. Every doctor is different, and if yours doesn't leave you feeling the way I felt, you should find another doctor to see. A good doctor will help you find a solution and give you the time and care that you deserve. I started medication that day, and it changed my mental health in ways I never expected. Although I had to go through many medication changes throughout my journey (a complication of having bipolar disorder), I still attribute medication to saving my life. Whether it's medication you need or something else, a medical professional can help you navigate those next steps that you need to take in order to be fully well.

4. BE HONEST WITH YOUR KIDS ABOUT YOUR MENTAL STATE.

Yep. This is a hard one. I used to hide my mental illness and struggles from my children. I felt like I needed to always put on a happy face for them, that I needed to always show them that I had it all together and was so strong. That feels like what we need to teach our kids, right? To be strong? But hiding your struggles and mental illness actually does the opposite. It shows your kids that if Mom doesn't struggle, then they must be broken if they are struggling. When we hide our struggles, we do nothing more than create an environment where our kids don't feel safe having their own range of emotions. Sadness, frustration, anger, impatience, and mental illness are all normal, and we need to stop the stigma of being anything less than happy. The more we talk to our kids about our own state, the more they understand and empathize when you are struggling. The less you mask your emotions, the more they learn about emotions. The more you talk to them about what you're going through, the less uncomfortable they will be when they get older if they struggle with their own mental health. Showing our true selves shows our true strength and shows our kids their own strength.

5. DON'T BE SO HARD ON YOURSELF.

No, I am not joking. I know it is a lot to ask. Being kinder to ourselves and more gentle, less judgmental, and less critical is hard. It takes a lot of changing and learning. It takes daily work and change. Being less critical of yourself means that every time you want to put yourself down for not making a homemade meal or leaving the dishes in the sink you instead choose kindness and accept that it is okay. I have taken years to start being kinder to myself. It wasn't easy to stop putting myself down and to stop speaking to myself in a negative way. It has taken a lot of effort. I have had to remind myself daily that I am a good mom, a good spouse, a strong woman. I have to tell myself that it is okay that I didn't get all the laundry done and that no one is upset with me about it except me. Every day I have to look at myself in the mirror and tell myself that I am doing a great job, that I am worthy, that I am loved.

Being kinder to myself is completely related to my next point.

6. PUT AWAY ALL YOUR SUPERMOM EXPECTATIONS.

In the time where social media is so prevalent in our daily lives, we all see the feeds of moms appearing to be supermoms. The homemade meals and snacks, the daily creative crafts and games, the homemade Valentine's Day cards and treats, the perfectly posed family photos . . . and we all get bombarded with this idea that that way is the way we are supposed to be as moms. But I promise you that it is not the way to being a great mom, spouse, homemaker, or woman. Being a supermom means loving your kids through all their ups and downs, giving them attention when they are behaving in undesirable ways, and supporting their dreams (even when those dreams are from your seven-year-old telling you she will own a Lamborghini before she is eighteen), because who are we to tear apart those big dreams? As a supermom, it is your job to love and care for YOURSELF so much that you have all the love in the world inside you to give to your baby when he wakes up every hour throughout the night. Being a supermom means being so kind to yourself and speaking so kindly to yourself that your kids learn to love themselves through watching you.

My instability with mental illness not only made an impact on my life, but it also made an impact on my kids' lives. If you take away anything from my story, take the motivation to manage your mental health now and stop waiting. Don't be like me and spend years in turmoil and damaging your kids, because not only is the guilt heart wrenching, but it takes years to undo the damage. I am still working on that healing with my children and within myself. But what you need to know is that there is hope for you. There is a better life, a happier life, a healthier life waiting for you. It isn't too late for you.

When we are struggling with mental illness, it feels as if it will stay that way forever, that the dark cloud will never lift from above our heads. But I can tell you that no matter how many times a dark cloud followed me around, it always lifted and the sun shone again. Now that I have sought help and have a strict self-care routine, I am able to go long periods with stability. I have limited bouts of depression, it's rare that I will go through mania, and my anxiety is under control. Thus, I have been able to maintain a healthy, happy, and successful lifestyle. But most importantly, I have been able to reconnect with my children and husband and create happy memories with them. To me, that alone is the true definition of successfully managing mental illness.

Koa Baker

Koa Baker stands out as a female executive in the male-dominated construction industry. Koa, along with her husband, founded Duffy Baker Construction Corp. Here, she takes on the role as Chief of Operations.

When Koa isn't opening doors and breaking glass ceilings in the business industry, she is pounding away on her computer writing books, blogs, and growing her Instagram following. Her reputation as an entrepreneur is well known, as her family was featured on the CBC television series *The Stats of Life—Working Life*. Koa is also a published author in the book *The Great Canadian Woman: She Is Strong and Free, Volume I*. Her chapter, "Becoming My Own Solution," discusses how to not only survive but thrive with a major mental illness diagnosis.

Koa's formal education came in the form of a bachelor's degree with a double major in Psychology and Indigenous Studies. Koa uses her education to help her better understand how to help men and women face and overcome their own adversity. Adversity is something Koa knows well. Before becoming an executive, author, and blogger, Koa had been lost, hopelessly adrift in a sea of abuse, trauma, limiting beliefs, and mental illness diagnoses. An unhappy combination of medication and booze kept her afloat. Through immense growth, Koa has taken on the belief that she was allowing all her adversity to take place, and in order to grow, she had to become her own solution. Now, Koa spends much of her time advocating for others who suffer with mental illness and normalizing it. She believes that those who suffer with mental illness shouldn't shrink themselves to fit the life of a sick person. Instead, mental illness can be embraced and accepted as a positive.

f KoaBaker

◙ @koabri

Thank you to my amazing husband for always standing by me, supporting me, encouraging me, and pushing me to be the best that I can be. You make everything about life brighter and more beautiful.

She Is

Creative

CHAPTER 3

CONNECTION THROUGH GREAT THINGS

Rebekah Jane Mersereau

It was Thanksgiving Day, and I was sitting at a group of tables brought together for the forty friends and family members who had gathered. I sat in wonder at the life that had brought me to this perfect moment, my son on my lap, my partner at our side, my son's six cousins and our friends and family nearby, the camp by the lake where our family could gather together, and the perfect home of our dreams from which we had just arrived. This was a moment to relish; it was picturesque, and a time to be everlastingly grateful for. I sat there seeing all this beauty in front of me and all I felt was defeat, lifelessness, and unfulfillment.

I asked myself, "How can I feel this way?" After our perfect feast, we drove home, and I cried the whole way. Where was that spark of life I had once felt? How had my life come to this? How could I not enjoy the most real and raw moments I had in front of me?

I had lost myself.

I always think back to a particular moment in my life. It was the end of high school, and I was in line at Starbucks where I struck up a conversation with a lady behind me. She asked me, "What do you want to do when you grow up?" This question is not an uncommon one for someone at the end of their high school career, so I was not surprised. I am sure I was bombarded by this question on a daily basis, but my unplanned answer to this woman made an impact on me. "Great things!" I told her, confidently. Shocked, she said, "And I believe you will." As I think back to this moment now, I know I had no clear goal and no agenda or restrictions for a life I was expected to lead. I simply had a creative path of wonder and adventure in front of me.

On this particular Thanksgiving, I asked myself if I was indeed doing great things. I was fortunate enough to be able to stay at home with my son, to have lived with my in-laws for a while when he was born, and to have unconditional support and love. I had helped so many children and families in my jobs, and I had created many paintings and sold most of them, some even being sent across the world. I had wanted to be a stay-at-home mom and be a good partner, and I had this. So why was I feeling so defeated and unfulfilled?

There was a feeling of needing something more nudging me, *urging me to create.*

I had been thinking about starting my own business, but I was not entirely sure what I was going to do. I found myself applying for start-up funding. I needed a business plan, so I decided to mix all my favourite things and things I was great at, especially art and working with children with disabilities, and put them all together and see where it took me. As the application process continued, my partner, rightly so, was concerned. What did this mean for our family, for our time together and our future? We saw the abundance of change and risk it was going to create in our lives and fear took over. I turned away from the business idea, I said no to the funding, and I found myself working part time at the job I said I wouldn't return to. It felt like the right choice, the smart choice.

It only took me a few weeks back in my job when I found myself at home, blank-minded, feeling absolutely nothing. I "woke up" in my living room, my son playing and laughing around me, and I was sitting like a useless blob on the floor. I realized that I did not want to feel this way, and it was not what I wanted to show my son a life should be like. That night in bed I cried. I told my partner I couldn't feel that way anymore and that I had made a huge mistake and my opportunity was lost. We wished together to have taken it all back.

In the nick of time, I applied again, just days away from my initial application expiring. I was accepted. We popped sparkling wine that night. I then promised that my family and our life together would come first and that I would be happier and more fulfilled. Then the spiral began—the spiral into that life we feared, the life we said no to in the first place.

Starting a business without a clear vision is daunting AF. I had no idea where I was going, what I was doing, or how I was going to do it. I had support in what I was about to create from every direction in life—from my friends and family—but in business, I heard crickets. The funding I received was supposed to dual as support in information and finances, but it ended up being a fight with no reward. I had few people to look up to, and many I knew had footsteps I did not want to follow. I found myself utterly alone in business.

This feeling of loneliness spread into my being. It infected me like a virus and contorted everything that I did. I had to prove to be a business worth noticing so others would respect me. I had to carry the weight of all ends of a business to stand. I had to hold myself together and get through the uproar of emotions that kept creeping in so I could work on my business. I had to figure it out on my own because there was no one else to help me do it.

As I started to pave a path in my business, I found myself surrendering to trivial things. This surrender left me unsure of what I had done each day and feeling just as unfulfilled as I had when I began, if not more so. My life during this time had few joys and celebrations. I became quick to anger, and I was bitter and spiteful in my home with my family. My garden, which I had tended to greatly the summer before, was near forgotten. I was still working at my job part time, and I was unable to show up fully for my clients. My home was cluttered with "work stuff." I spent less and less time with my son and partner. I saw myself from an outside view, watching myself run things into the ground. I truly wanted to appreciate the summer months, but all I could focus on was working and making it to the inevitable autumn, which was when I had decided, without proof, that I would be able to support myself in this half-created business.

When autumn came, my work and obsession with this undefined vision of "success" was still holding me in a crazed state. I was unshakable and drowning. I held onto my loneliness, and any momentum of success was immediately met with another thing to work toward. I had forgotten myself and said I would find her again when I was able to create the time.

Fast-forward to the last days of 2019. My nearly one-year-old business was nowhere where I had wanted it to be, and I felt like a failure. Determined not to let December 2020 feel the same, I opened myself up to real possibility and healing. I met Sarah Swain and she quoted Cassie Jeans: "To elevate, we must first heal." I looked at her, and she might not have even noticed the pure shock and horror on my face as she dropped the biggest truth bomb on me. How could it have been so obvious and so lost on me all year? I didn't say anything to her, but I was ashamed and heartbroken because I felt like I had wasted my entire year building more and more walls around me, and for what?

I didn't let that shame stop me; it only inspired me.

I started breaking down walls and accepting the reality of my anger and work obsession that had been building up and bubbling inside. I began my self-healing. I didn't do it alone, though; I found people to help me. I talked to my partner, and I opened up to my family and friends. I asked for help, I allowed help, I *chose* help.

No one could be prepared for what was to come in 2020.

As COVID-19 emerged, I felt the recycling of feeling bubbling up again as I was smacked in the face with the constant pivots, the time, the new life of isolation. I had to sit back and assess what was happening and how I was going to manage within it. Fear started to take over me, but I quickly realized that this time was an opportunity for growth and making a difference in my life and business. I know that people saw what I was doing and applauded how great and perfect I seemed to have flawlessly transitioned into the new life of COVID-19, but I was the first to admit that it was anything but calm. I was scared and unsure. It was a crazy roller coaster of emotions on a weekly, daily, and hourly basis. However, I recognized the difference a year had made in my life. If COVID-19 had emerged in 2019, I am honestly scared to think of how I would have handled it; it probably would have been a nightmare of explosive emotions and feelings of defeat. Thankfully, I had already committed myself to the healing and growth process. Though the roller coaster was very present, I was able to assess, practice gratitude, and utilize this time as an opportunity for personal development.

Finding my new balance was not easy. It did not happen overnight; it took months, and truthfully, it is still a work in progress. I was able to take my time, take a step back and assess what is important—what my family, my business, and I needed from me. I finally allowed myself to start seeing what was necessary for all the aspects in my life to work cohesively instead of hustling myself silly. Looking back, it seems so obvious now to see my life as equally important compartments that need attention, support, and care; my business would not fix me, it was just a part of what supported me and helped me grow, but only if I took care of myself holistically.

I said yes to my mental health, and this was no small feat. I had held onto unaddressed trauma my entire life, so saying yes was a grand start but opened up what felt like a never-ending path of uncovering. The trauma I held onto was inaudible, unthinkable, and unbearable for me. I held it deep within a cellular level. With help from my partner, my therapist, and the other incredible people I surrounded myself with, I was able to turn the trauma into actionable healing—a lifelong process. I learned to accept my story and delve into vulnerability.

My story begins before I was born. I have a genetic bone disorder called Osteogenesis Imperfecta Type 1, which is a lack of collagen that causes low bone density and therefore, brittle bones. Starting in utero where I broke my femur and up until high school, I had around fifty-five fractures. During adolescence, fractures are more prominent, and after a person is done growing, fractures become infrequent or cease all together. I am currently twenty-six years old and haven't had a fracture in nine years. When I was young, my life felt "normal" because it was all I had known. I knew I was different because I recognized that others weren't like me and my family. They weren't broken like I was. I normalized being the broken ones. Normalcy was exactly what it was, living through many traumatic events within my own body and those of my family members. In the calm of adulthood, why would I assume to address the "normalcy" of what I had been through? I got through the battlefield that was my childhood; I came out strong, independent, victorious. Little did I know then that this physical trauma had been carefully stored within each of my cells. *To ignore my story is to ignore my entire being.*

"Your story is something that happened to you, not what defines you." - Emily Gough

My story is what is biologically me, but it does not define me. It helped me become who I am today and who I am growing to be. The problem was that I couldn't accept my story, I did not want my story to define me, and I was scared to admit or address the trauma because if I did, it could take over me. This was very true in the moment; the fear and anxiety were taking over me but I didn't need to let it. When I accepted my story as a lot of things that happened to me and not as something that defines me, I was able to grow, learn, and "rumble with vulnerability," as Brené Brown says.[1] Hiding away from my story held me back in my own personal development, in my relationships, and in my business.

It makes perfect sense that I was so angry, so unfulfilled, and so addicted to my business. Hiding from your story, your very cells, is exhausting work.

Working in and growing through my business helped me understand my mental health and create connections through my creativity. This fact is laughable in a way because it is literally what my program is called: "Connections through Creativity." But my program was made for other people, not for me. Funny how things work out, isn't it? The more I taught creativity, the more I learned about myself, and not just creatively but in a deeply healing way. I reaffirmed that connecting ourselves through creativity is healing, which is my soul's purpose.

When I heard people talk about values, I didn't understand how they could choose something and stick with it; my creative mind couldn't handle the pressure of one thing. Then I discovered Brené Brown. Her directions were simple: here's a list, choose two. Somehow, it was that simple and that powerful. I chose three core values: joy, growth, and making a positive difference. Now I live by them. If my actions in life and business do not produce joy, growth, or make a positive difference, then they are not worth my time. This "simple act" of living in my values held me accountable to my personal development and mental health. I thought I was on the right track, but now when I go to do something, I can check in with myself and *know* I am.

Joy is living presently in the moments that we have now; practice joy and the rest will follow. This is my mantra for living a joyful life. I had an epiphany one day. I realized that I was trying to search for joy and happiness by fixing the things around me. My boyfriend, Thomas, lives and breathes joy and always says, "Just be happy!" And I used to say, "That's easier said than done." He is absolutely right, though. It took me this long to see it. I was trying to fix everything backwards; my goal was to be happy, and I thought I had to fix all the things around me in order to achieve this joy. But no, it's the opposite. Practice joy, like Thomas, and the rest will follow.

Growth is having an open mind to learning, experiencing, and creating a better tomorrow. There is a quote by Steve Maraboli that goes something like "To plant a seed is to believe in a better tomorrow." That is growth. It might seem insignificant to plant a seed, but at harvest time, when we are overflowing with produce, it needs to be shared. This belief links into another saying: "You can't give from an empty cup." If we don't plant enough seeds or provide them with the right soil, our cup will remain empty. To care for your seeds, your garden, your personal development is to have growth, and so much so that there is enough to share at feasts. Stagnation is the opposite of growth, and honestly, it hurts more than acting in a growth mindset, so why not dive into growth? If I kept at what I was doing, I would be worse off, stewing in anguish. If I keep an open mind to learning, to experiencing and understanding my own and other's experiences, I create a better tomorrow. My growth will not just make an impact on and benefit me but also those around me who I care enough to share it with as well.

Making a positive difference includes taking many small intentional actions that add up to create change and greater impact for myself and others. Creating change can feel like a huge undertaking, but I break it down into many, many small acts that create a big difference. This breaking down creates manageable expectations for myself and leads me on the path that I know is right. I think back to my younger self standing in that Starbucks line telling a stranger that I was going to do great things. I am and I will continue to do so if I take small steps to making a positive difference in my life to support me, my friends, my family, my clients, and those I might never meet but are positively affected by what I create in my lifetime. These puzzle pieces of my life connect together: this perfect snapshot of my life at Thanksgiving, lost and broken in my life, creating my business, the trauma my body holds. They are my story. They are what is leading me into my "great things" I prophesied for

THE GREAT CANADIAN WOMAN

myself at age seventeen. It took me ten years to understand what I meant in that Starbucks line. To live in my values of joy, growth, and making a difference, to accept healing, to take chances and dare to be courageous and strong, to let my cup overflow—these create a life full of great things. My definition of great things isn't a clear answer I can provide you with; instead, it will be a series of things as I am living a full life and being present.

My story is just beginning. I have many more tales to share, many more lessons to learn, much more healing to accept and experiences to create. I understand that this is a lifelong journey, and I am excited for everything to come. And honestly, I am quite scared. But I know everything I create and everything I learn and experience will be worth it. My story is just beginning; to be continued.

Rebekah Jane Mersereau

Rebekah Jane Mersereau, (she/her), is an Inclusive Community Art Instructor, Community Director, Creative, Mom, Business Owner, and Canadian. She spent a long time wondering how she could make a positive impact through her own business. She didn't know how or believe that she already had the skill set to make a meaningful difference. Little did she know at the time that by taking her passion, experience, and expertise that she would be creating a radical impact for her community. She quickly realized that her power for impact was far greater than one person in one small town could do, which is where "Connections through Creativity" was born.

Rebekah is a proud mom of a happy boy, Cooper, who makes everyone laugh every day and is learning how to explore his own creativity alongside both his parents. Rebekah lives in rural New Brunswick with her partner (Thomas), Cooper, and their two cats, Zera and Fidel. They acquired a fantastic yard full of life in their beautiful home that they love to tend to. In the summertime on the deck or winter by the fire, you can find Rebekah sitting down with a nice cup of tea, coffee, or cider with a good book. After Cooper was born, reading children's literature has become one of her favourite pastimes with him. They both love reading books, spending time at the library, and trying to carry all the said books home. What Rebekah loves most about everything she does is sharing it with her son and seeing him learn, grow, and explore.

🌐 rebekahjaneart.ca

🌐 etsy.com/ca/shop/RebekahJaneArt

f RebekahJaneArt

in @RebekahJaneArt

📷 @RebekahJaneArt

I want to thank everyone from the bottom of my heart who has been a part of this journey with me: all of my family, friends, my mastermind, and my counsellor.

A special thank you to Thomas, Kate, and Cooper, my Super Cooper. Kate, my dear friend, you believe in me like no other and have helped me work through this huge growth process every step of the way (with our toddlers "whirlwinding" around us!). Thomas, my love, you have supported me through the huge roller coaster ride in our life and business, through thick and thin; if we can get through everything we have in these short years, there's nothing we can't handle. You remind me every day to live life fully, to work hard, and to do it with all the love, cuddles, play, and joy one can muster. Cooper, my baby, you have kept me grounded and taught me what living life should be. You have always been equally enthusiastic to help me and tell me when I need to stop and play. Mommy couldn't be prouder of the little man you're growing up to be. You, too, will do great things.

She Is

——— Loving

CHAPTER 4

LOVE, MARRIAGE, EMPTY CARRIAGE

Amanda Stewart

We all have this perception of what our future will look like, or what we want it to look like. We dream of whom we will marry and the house we will live in with our beautiful, well-behaved children. Everyone's dreams of their future vary, but they usually look something like this: I will fall in love with the person of my dreams in a foreign land, somewhere romantic like Paris or Italy. We will look each other in the eyes and just know it was meant to be. We will have a gloriously perfect wedding, and all our family and friends will be in awe of our love. We will then be blessed with X number of beautiful, happy, and healthy kids and will live happily ever after in our white-picket-fenced home. Sound about right? Well, most of this story is true in my case. When I was eighteen and not in any way searching for eternal love, I met this amazing man with whom I was working at our local hardware store. I know what you're thinking: Wow! Eighteen, and the local hardware store is nowhere near Paris. But I knew he was the one. We dated while I went off to college and he stayed back home as he is six years my senior and had already finished college and was buying his first house. When I graduated from nursing school and began my first job in my career in nursing, we had been dating for five years so it's easy to say we were serious and planning our futures together. We moved in together, and on a beautiful and sunny Easter morning in 2014, he asked me the big question: "Will you marry me?" I only had one answer, and of course it was yes!

On September 12, 2015, I put on a stunning cream-coloured lace dress with my mom and two best friends beside me. I was so excited to begin my journey with the man with whom I was so absolutely in love. Walking down the church aisle with friends and family staring at me, all I could see and focus on was the man before me. He wore a black suit and a crisp white shirt with a black bow tie that suited him so well. He was so handsome, so manly, with big blue eyes, sandy blond hair, and a sleek, manly stature; I wondered what our kids would look like. After the "I do's" and the reception, we went back to our place. Now most couples fly off to the honeymoon right after the wedding or spend the night at a luxurious hotel for their wedding night. Unfortunately, Shawn (my husband) and I found during our wedding planning and engagement that we did not have the best support system. So, off to our humble home it was for us, and we planned to expand our new family as soon as possible. I always knew getting pregnant would be a struggle (as family history would indicate), so as happy and excited that I was to expand my new family with the man I love, I knew it was not going to be a smooth ride. Shawn and I always kept lines of communication open. I never hid anything from him, so he knew prior to us tying the knot that things may not go as planned.

A year went by with us having fun, enjoying the "honeymoon phase," and enjoying each other's company (wink, wink!). But that blissful phase soon turned into overwhelming feelings of fear, doubt, concern, frustration, and worry. With lots of trying and still no positive pregnancy tests, it was time to make that phone call to the OB/GYN to get some answers. Months and months went by with invasive tests, procedures, blood work, and visits to doctors, dieticians, nurse practitioners, and the OB/GYN, etc., only to have the words "sorry to tell you, you are not ovulating" hit me like a ton of bricks. You are not ovulating? What does that even mean? How could I not be ovulating? I'm a woman! What did that mean for us? Was it my fault? What did I do wrong? Would my husband still love me? Would he blame me? What are our options? There were so many questions going through my head. We were blessed with an amazing OB/GYN, who was patient and kind. He sat us down and went through all the options we had in detail, everything from medication, procedures, to further testing. Knowing that my husband was fertile and I was the cause of this delay in our future was heartbreaking. I am so thankful we had that open line of communication so I could express my guilt and fears. People always say blame should not be placed on one particular party in these situations, but my deep knowing that I was the root cause, that I was at fault because of my lack of proper body function was enough to have me spiralling into a deep depression. My husband, my rock and support, was so loving, and he continued to reassure me that this situation was a mountain we would climb and face together.

As couples close to us were quickly expanding their families and announcing their pregnancies, our infertility felt like a knife to the heart. I remember one day so clearly. A family member and his spouse arrived at my back door. They came into our home and told me with a smile on their faces and excitement in their eyes that they were celebrating something special: their first pregnancy. I was in shock. I was happy for them and simultaneously devastated for us. My emotions were battling it out inside of me like two rabid beasts fighting over meat. I was trying so hard to put a smile on my face, but the tears kept trying to push through. After saying the congratulations, I just wanted the happy couple out of my home, out of my personal space, my sanctuary, my place of peace and safety, so I could curl up in a ball on the floor and cry.

Some people knew about our struggles and heartache, and while some were very sensitive to the issue, others were not. How do you put on a fake smile and say congratulations to someone when you have been heartbroken and emotionally exhausted from trying to do something that others find so easy to do? The absolute hardest thing to hear was "it was only our second month of trying." The medication I was prescribed can only be taken for six months; after six months, other options must be considered. After months of medication that made me physically ill, stressed, emotional, and lethargic, it was looking as though it was time to lose hope. I was at the point in my life when I was then trying to grieve and find acceptance in the fact that a child may not be in our future, our prayers may not be answered, and the one thing I wanted oh so badly in life I may never get. I even gave my husband an out—I gave him an opportunity to close the door on our marriage and find another wife who could give him what I could not. I know what you're probably thinking . . . What? But I love him and the thought of him not having the future he envisioned for himself was too painful for me to bear. I was honest with him and told him I understood children were something we both wanted, so I completely understood if he wanted to leave the relationship. I still clearly remember the conversation. I remember him looking at me with those big blue eyes, wrapping me up in a big loving hug that always made me feel so small and so safe, giving me a kiss on the forehead as he often does, and telling me he wasn't going anywhere. He was here to stay. Children or no children. Through the good and the bad, happy and sad. We were going to continue the climb up the mountain together.

It was a Thursday afternoon in June when I came across a pregnancy test in our bathroom. It was still in the package, never opened or used, and I was keeping this test by chance I would need it. I had this strange instinct that I didn't want to just throw out a perfectly good (and expensive) pregnancy test, so in the midst of cleaning, I took the test. As I had taken many pregnancy tests before, all having the same result of negative, I thought why would this one be any different? But it was. On that Thursday, I finally got to read the word **pregnant** on a test. Pregnant one to two weeks. Saying I was crazy emotional is putting it lightly. I mean I was ugly crying, and when I instinctively called my mom, she pulled her car over because she thought I had injured myself or someone had died. As my mom and I were both hysterical (and it is safe to say that we were both ugly crying at this point), I knew I had to tell Shawn right away. I knew I couldn't keep this surprise from him, even if I tried! I saw many cute pregnancy announcements using ultrasound pictures and baby bumps, but as much as I was keeping track of menstruation, ovulation, diet change, medication, and so on, I knew Shawn was too—maybe not to the extent I was, but he would have known. I immediately drove to the dealership where Shawn was working at the time, waited for him to get on his break and broke the news. Seeing the shock on his face was priceless. I could tell he needed some time to process the news that he was going to be a dad. While still processing the new information, and through the excitement and emotions of happiness and joy, we couldn't help but worry as the pregnancy was still new and early. It's crazy to think one out of four pregnancies results in miscarriage. That is one in four that are reported, anyway. That statistic doesn't include those not reported or chemical pregnancies or pregnancies resulting in early loss. There is this torn feeling between the initial excitement of wanting to share the news and start buying baby clothes and products but also having that fear and concern in the back of your mind. Those "what ifs" always remain in your thoughts.

So, the test showed positive . . . now what? Now, because I am a health care provider myself, you must be thinking, "Well, you must have some idea of what's coming up, and what to do, where to go, who to see, and so on." Um, nope. My area of practice is in surgical and geriatrics, and I have no specialized training in obstetrics. I was relying solely on the information and trust from fellow health care workers and their teams. Thankfully, I was under the care of many amazing people, but the emotions and fear were still there. Anytime I felt some extra leakage down south, I rushed to the ladies' room, praying not to see blood. I cried and prayed over every cramp I felt, hoping things wouldn't take a turn for the worse. Mind you, during this time I was also working three jobs. I know, I know, not a smart thing to do while pregnant. Luckily enough, I had some amazing bosses at the zoo where I worked and a lot of great co-workers at my nursing job. But be it as it may, the physical, emotional, and mental strain I was encountering at my nursing job was very toxic. I spent most of my shift protecting my tiny baby bump from being kicked, punched, or hit by patients or bumping into medical carts, wheelchairs, walkers, etc. Eight- to twelve-hour shifts on my feet with maximum of one "break" were strenuous, but thankfully, my little peanut put up with the strain this momma was putting it under.

I always dreamed of being a mom, and it was finally going to happen. After our fertility struggles, I was so excited to grow a baby bump! I couldn't wait to have a baby belly and have that glow that you see in so many pregnant women. I didn't get to have that, though. I looked sick and pale, and I was lethargic and oily, with acne spreading all over my face, neck, back, and shoulders. The pregnancy belly just looked as though I ate too many burgers that day. It was so hard because my joy of being pregnant was constantly being tested by the comments and snickers from other women. I stayed focused though, because my health and our desire to deliver our baby safely after a tough pregnancy was our great-est goal. After our crazy fertility struggles and a wild pregnancy, we were blessed with a miracle baby via Caesarean at thirty-two weeks gestation—a beautiful, 3 lb., 3 oz. baby boy with golden brown hair and big blue eyes that would one day change to rich dark brown.

Hubby and I decided three months after the birth of our son

that we would try again for another baby. We knew that fertility was already a struggle for us, so we thought we would get a jump-start on the next. We always envisioned having two kids. After the emotional turmoil of getting pregnant the first time, we thought the second time around would be easier, right? Right? Boy, were we wrong. You always hear about people struggling to have one, then getting pregnant quickly with a second, or about parents who are surprised by a second when they weren't even planning for another. We were very thrilled to get started, though. Having our kiddos close together in age was something we were hopeful for but not set on, and that's a good thing too. Jack (our son) turned one, and I was still not pregnant. Back to fertility clinics, IUI treatments, injections, medication, routine visits, follow-ups, testing, and so much more. A year later, and nothing. This infertility not only created a sense of disappointment but a whole different level of sadness and stress. The comments started again: "Jack needs a sibling; when are you going to have another?" And when we did explain our struggles, the comment that bit the most was "well, at least you have one." I am so thankful for my miracle child, and I cannot express how much I love my son, but when you have a vision and a goal to have more children, to think you may have to give that up (and add on not having support outside your own marital relationship) is beyond hurtful. There is a grieving process. Getting invited to parties and couples announcing their pregnancies felt like a slap in the face. The envy nearly destroyed me. To see others being able to get pregnant when they wanted, to have as many children as they wanted without any fertility struggles, was very difficult to process. As happy as I was for them, it's an internal struggle that's hard to put into words.

I found it incredibly hard to find happiness for couples who included me in their announcements when they knew the struggles my husband and I were going through with pregnancy and fertility. But what were they supposed to do? Exclude me? My thoughts were always, "Why did you invite me here? Why would you think I would want to come here?" as if it were some sort of personal attack against me. It was very difficult to hold back the tears and put on a brave face in the same way it was hard the first time we were trying. It just hurt so much and no one seemed to understand. I started losing faith, hope, and confidence, as well as relationships and family. My pain was at the wheel and all I could think about was why not me? What are they doing that I am not doing? Why them and not us? I obsessively reviewed diets, lifestyle, stress levels, etc. We eventually decided to move to another province to detach ourselves from everything that caused us pain, sadness, and grief. We wanted to give our son the best life possible and create the optimal environment to live in and continue to try and expand our family.

I consider myself and my husband to be fairly healthy. I do not smoke or drink, I live an active life, and I eat healthfully with the occasional chocolate bar as a treat. Hubby has the occasional drink, doesn't smoke, and lives an active life. So, what were we doing wrong? The guilt of not being able to get pregnant continued to eat me alive. The struggle for pregnancy constantly tested our faith and hope. I'm not a perfect parent, but my son (who is autistic) is everything, and we have dedicated our lives to making sure he has all he needs. I just wanted to receive what so many others were able to have so freely, easily, and without much effort. I really didn't think that was much to pray for, but it felt like I must have been asking for the world. After two and a half years of fertility struggles, two failed IUI treatments, months of medication (which again made me incredibly sick), 229 needles, and monthly blood work, we got pregnant. I thought it was too good to be true. After the joy and tears and an additional ultrasound, we discovered that the baby was not developing properly, and my body began to reject the pregnancy. It took two and a half years of trying everything in our power, combined with heartache and disappointment with every month of "not pregnant," and in the end I lost my baby (Lola Fleurette). I wish I could put into words how I felt and continue to feel about losing a child, but honestly, there are no words. The unthinkable had happened. How were we going to recover? Would we be okay?

We chose to keep trying. We often do not like to talk about fertility, miscarriage, infant loss, etc., because it is the hardest thing a couple will go through. The mental and emotional pain is unlike any other. Your intimate relationship is no longer spontaneous or romantic, but rather timed, calculated, and the next thing to a crazy science experiment trying to win the championship cup. Between all the different hormone surges, pee sticks, different "seed-helping" lubricants, yoga positions, and crazy nutritional supplements, you would think we would at least get the first-place prize at the science fair.

To this day I reflect on our fertility struggles with a mixture of heartache and gratitude. These struggles have tried to take so much from me: family, relationships, and even physical locations. But I will never let it take my hope and faith. This journey of infertility has shown me how to advocate for myself, for other women, and to show other women and couples they are not alone. It has given me the strength to reflect on my life purpose and what/who I want to be in it. It has given me the strength to say no to people and toxic situations to keep my life and environment as fruitful and healthy as I can. Most of all, our fertility struggle has shown me our support system: who has been there for us and who did not have the courage or love to support us through our climb. My journey of infertility, pregnancy loss, and pregnancy may seem small to those who have been trying for ten years, twelve years, even fifteen-plus years; however, it has allowed me to value what is really important in life and to not take what may be considered "the little things" for granted. What may come as something easy and simple to some may be a life-changing struggle to others. Some may find pregnancy a breeze, and for others, it may be something they will never get to experience. It has opened my eyes and has changed my life, to say the least. When you live in a world of Ross and Rachels, and you're Monica and Chandler, understand you are not alone: there are others out there who can relate and empathize.

I said I would never let infertility take my hope and faith. And on September 27, 2020, our little girl, Noella Fleur Stewart, was born at 5 lbs., 7 oz.

Amanda Stewart

With a résumé ranging from working at a zoo to practical nursing, Amanda Stewart has a wide variety of skills and knowledge. Amanda is a dedicated mom to an amazing autistic little boy and a baby girl. Amanda is the wife to a downright amazing guy and has a soft spot in her heart for animals. She is an accomplished nurse with more than six years' experience and has built a reputation for being caring, supportive, and honest. Embracing the core values of integrity, innovation, and growth, Amanda understands the true value of the little things, turning her own story of struggle into a tale of inspiration, strength, and hope.

After a few bumps in the road, Amanda has steered her focus from her nursing career to devoting her time and energy to family and home life. Caring, empathetic, and passionate have always been strong characteristics to describe Amanda, characteristics that she invests into her family and hobby farm. Amanda can be found volunteering and fundraising for her son's daycare and various activities for Autism Nova Scotia or in the barn caring for her rescue animals. Amanda takes great pride in caring for her family and animals, ensuring they have the love and support they deserve.

To my husband, Shawn, with whom I could not have flourished into the person I am today. You have given me strength, support, and unconditional love during this crazy journey. To my beautiful children, both by my side and in heaven (Jack, Lola, and Noella).

This chapter is dedicated to all the women out there who have struggled and continue to struggle with pregnancy/fertility: you are strong, fierce, and not alone.

Many thanks to The Great Canadian Woman for letting me share my story (Sarah Swain), and of course, to Jackie VanderLinden who kept me on track to complete this chapter on time.

She Is

Intuitive

CHAPTER 5

SOCIAL WORK BURNOUT TO SPIRITUAL BREAKOUT

Lindsay Anderson

As I reflected on my story over the past couple of years, I came to understand that there were two major untruths that I'd been swallowing. Delicious untruths my ego savoured. They had been so deeply ingrained that I had come to accept them, without question.

The first untruth: I need to have the answers . . . all of them, right now.

The second untruth: I am solely responsible for creating alignment and purpose in my life.

These lies created an illusion of control that resulted in any "failure" leaving me feeling unworthy, unloved, and just plain not good enough. Thus, this became the narrative I've carried throughout my entire life—that I'm not good enough. Not a good enough friend, wife, daughter, writer, employee, etc.

It wasn't until my world came crashing down around me that my ego, for that snapshot second, recognized that it didn't have the answers. The safety net it had created was no longer viable, and so began my soul-searching journey. Something within me had been stirred. An unrelenting surge, an undeniable thirst, an itch that demanded a scratch. There was no going back. It was time for these two lies to rear their ugly heads, fully seen and fully felt. It was time for my world to shift into place. Time for me to fully embrace my spiritual purpose, uncover my deepest shadows, and learn the difficult lessons of surrender and alignment in my personal, professional, and spiritual life.

*　*　*

I was a bossy kid; let's get that right out in the open. A natural-born leader with ALL the answers. As I got older, this deep need to have the answers began manifesting as anxiety and panic attacks. When things would start to veer off path, when I didn't know what to expect next, when I couldn't see the solution, when I didn't get my way, I would feel a complete loss of control. Fear was a go-to and, admittedly, was the deciding factor for most of the choices I made. I trusted the untruths. I micromanaged the Universe in every capacity of my life.

My human brain could not grasp the complexities of the Universe—that it was weaving, shifting, and moving things around me. That it didn't need my permission to do any of it, and that it certainly didn't need my advice. So, I pushed against the grain in almost everything that I did.

And here's the thing . . . as we're trying to micromanage what goes on here, we become stuck in this perpetual cycle of ego-feeding frenzy. A consistent struggle of scarcity, anxiety, fear, depression, restlessness, and these nasty little narratives. When we push against the grain, we slip into the nail-biting stress of obsessing with the "whys" and believing that we are solely responsible for creating alignment, success, and happiness in this lifetime. We do everything we can to force our will. We live by the illusion of control.

And let's be real . . . if we were in charge of aligning our lives, that would imply that we know what's best, which would also imply that we have all of the answers.

And we don't.

When we believe we do, we (in my father's words) tend to get a "swift kick in the ass." A swift kick, directly from the Universe.

Let's rewind a little and give this story the girth it needs to resonate with you. Yes, my story is MY story. Keep an open mind, let the lessons weasel their way in and spark something in your soul. Take what you need (or at least what your soul is craving) and leave the rest on these pages. This is a story for the womxn who are stuck in the roundabout of mediocrity and "shoulds." The

THE GREAT CANADIAN WOMAN

womxn who are craving more. The womxn who keep short-ending themselves (dead-end relationships, jobs that don't excite them, the never-ending list of hobbies that don't quite hit the spot) because they are (or have been) unwilling to look honestly at their obsession with control.

This story is about me, for you. Because I chose to surrender, to stop fighting against the Universe and start working WITH it. I chose to take the leap and clear the path so that you can feel safe to do the same. Because I finally grasped that perhaps letting go of these lies was the key to creating conscious harmony with the Universe and starting to live the life I was truly meant to live.

* * *

NOVEMBER 2017

Here I am, sitting on my couch, ready to throw my work phone across the room. Friday afternoons in social work were always the worst and got increasingly unhealthier as my burnout progressed. Social work was the perfect shadow-calling for someone like me. The halfway mark between my soul-calling and a mediocre life. I had an interview earlier in the day for a management position, and I was desperate for it. This new position was the light at the end of my big burnout tunnel. I had been working in a position that "should" have been a perfect fit, but the fact that I'm an incredibly sensitive empath was not contributing to the overall level of job satisfaction or mental well-being. I misread the depression, the avoidance, the withdrawal, the lack of enjoyment in literally every-thing, the headaches and the body aches, or perhaps I just chose to push them aside because *that was life*. I was happy (*enough*). I was living with my partner, my parents were proud of me, I made a good paycheque. On paper it looked like I had it all together, but I was miserable, and the worst part was that I was lying to everyone about it, including myself.

The next morning, I sat on this same couch listening to my partner admit they cheated on me the night before. The Friday to follow, work disclosed they chose someone else for the job.

I had never felt more rejected in my entire life. *WHY was this happening TO ME?!* Why did I deserve this? What could she (the other woman and the co-worker) offer that I couldn't? What was wrong with me? Why wasn't I good enough?! I couldn't wrap my head around any of it. Everything was ruined. My life was falling apart. My partner cheating was confusing for sure, but I was lit-erally destroyed about the job. I felt like getting that job would have fixed everything. I felt like it was completely in alignment with where I wanted to go and who I wanted to be.

I was all-in with a twenty-million-dollar poker hand. And I just LOST. Everything was crumbling around me. I was drowning with no room to breathe. I felt it deeply. Deeper than I had ever felt anything before. I ugly-cried for days, and I still shudder now as

I share my truth—my truth that I contemplated both self-harm and suicide. But I didn't want to die. I wanted to live a different life. I didn't want to be me anymore, and I had no clue who "me" even was. I was shaken to my core, and for the first time in my life, I didn't have the answers. Nor did I have the capacity to try. I was in full-blown FEAR. I was no longer the little girl who had all the answers. I was the thirty-year-old woman begging for help and crying for guidance. I didn't even have the capacity to be embarrassed or insecure about it.

For a period of time, I surrendered. I surrendered to my parents' support, my family doctor's advice, my therapist, my spiritual mentor, and even my partner. Ultimately, it was their suggestion that led me to a silent retreat where I started opening up and leaning into the notion that the Universe had ultimate control here. This knowledge was uncomfortable and disorienting. It was the moment I tuned into my soul and gave it space to exist in this lifetime. The next couple of weeks I attended countless therapy appointments, saw my doctor weekly, started antidepressants, took a medical leave of absence, and hibernated in my apartment. Admitting I didn't know what was best for me was excruciating. But the alternative was so, so much worse. I had a purpose here, and although the spark was very dim, it was lit.

On January 4, 2018, my partner disclosed their continued relationship with the other woman. It was really over. The last mountain that had to fall. The final element of "normalcy" that

I gripped to was taken. Everything, and I mean everything that was no longer in alignment with my highest purpose, had fallen away—and without my permission. I felt empty. And so, my journey from Social Work Burnout to Spiritual Breakout truly began. I had nothing, a clean slate, and somehow, I trusted in the beauty of a fresh start.

Tokens of Truth

As humans, we introduce items/people/careers/situations in our lives that we truly believe are in alignment. Our understanding of this belief is often based on years of untruths and ego-driven narratives, and for this reason, we need to trust in the crumble.

When things go wrong, **hold space for yourself** and feel every emotion as sacred. Things will not be processed or healed if you are unwilling to experience them in their fullest capacity. You are only extending the pain by repressing it.

Asking for help is crucial to success. No one ever became successful and happy on their own.

Your ego is not your enemy. Befriending your ego, cultivating a relationship where you have an understanding of where it is coming from, is an integral part of trusting your soul.

2018

I spent most of 2018 wrapped up in my best friends' arms. I was doing all the things and felt safe to feel into the process of healing. I had created a very small cocoon of safety around me, which included my parents and brother, my best friend and her children, and a new partner. The children brought joy to my life when I was numb. I was very lucky to have people hold space so graciously as I learned to put the pieces of my life together.

As I started to feel better, my ego weaseled its way back in. It needed to regain control, to provide answers, and to be validated. I spent countless sleepless nights obsessing about returning to work. Most days I was convinced that the position I held was not healthy for me, so I sat with every other option available. I remember one morning at 4:00, flipping between twelve different tabs on my phone and thinking, "Wow! This is exactly how busy my brain feels." I was on a frenzied search to find something that might interest me, and when nothing did, I would focus on the jobs that were "somewhat" interesting or that would at least bring in a decent paycheque.

Let's face it—our job defines us in many ways. Next to knowing your name, people want to know what you do. Our value and purpose in this world are based on how we are received professionally. Therefore, our desire to provide answers that impress and claim our purpose is very high, and very unhealthy. In a success- and power-driven society, your occupation is held in esteem, and these perceptions sit very heavily in our culturally created and wounded ego. If we aren't making money, we immediately carry the narrative that we aren't valuable, that we can't contribute, and that we aren't good enough—yet another untruth.

Naturally, I had fallen back into the trap of relentlessly needing to know the answers and forcing control in my life. I can't say I was all that surprised when serendipitously, things would happen to prevent me from returning to work as I entertained all that was not in alignment with my highest purpose. Things would happen that would throw me into deep healing.

In February my grandpa was admitted to palliative care. He was ninety-seven and still head over heels in love with my grandma, even after sixty-seven years of marriage. I had the opportunity to bring my grandma to the hospital to visit him during this time. This was my first major lesson around how the Universe was cultivating alignment in my life, despite how obsessive I was toward my own will. This was just one of the reasons I needed to be off work; one of the reasons that I wasn't resonating with any job that appeared in my search; one of the reasons that my doctor cancelled two appointments in a row to complete my return-to-work paperwork. I don't think I could ever put into words how much it meant to me to spend this time with my grandparents. These two months showed me what REAL love is: butterflies after sixty-seven years of marriage. My grandpa passed away at the end of March, and again, the Universe guided me toward extending my leave and sinking deeper into my recovery.

I became quite cyclical. A teeter-totter of force and flow. I would surrender to the process, allowing myself to rest, heal in the discomfort and explore everything about myself and then I would crave "normalcy" and exert my will. I thought I might return to social work in either case management or an administrative role; I thought maybe I would start serving at a restaurant or work in retail. But every single time that I would look at these options, something would happen that would prevent it to the point that I ended up moving from a psychological leave of absence to a physical leave of absence when I was referred to an oncology program for cancer cells on my cervix.

I was being ordered to stay still, to look within, to feel into the healing, to allow, to learn to trust—both the Universe and myself—and having my grandpa's spirit guiding me made surrendering just a little bit easier. *Cool note:* The moment I finished writing these words, the clock read 3:33 p.m. and the song "From the Ground Up" by Dan + Shay started. This song reminds me very deeply of my grandparents. Here I am, sitting in the middle of Starbucks, smiling and crying. And all I can think is that "this is exactly what 2018 felt like." Smiling and crying. A serious mishmash of raw emotion and spiritual awakening. Being stripped completely naked and, at the same time, being held so firm.

Ultimately, I made good use of the stillness the Universe was cultivating for me. This is a piece of my journey that is incredibly personal, because what I was drawn to, and what you might be, will vary significantly, I'm sure. Where we are pulled isn't what matters. It's that we allow ourselves to trust and be led. I allowed my soul to be guided. I consciously and intentionally created space for this guiding. Whatever you are drawn to, this part of your journey is crucial. Allowing your soul to be ignited is vital. Dismissing societal pressure and unhealthy narratives and getting to know yourself and what you stand for is the only way you will ever truly cultivate joy, success, and purpose in this lifetime, no matter what that looks like for you.

My journey consisted of psychotherapy, reiki, antidepressants, group meditation, rigorous inner child and shadow work, online courses, massage therapy, journaling, womxn's circles, sacred spaces, reading, crystals, oracle cards, lakefront serenity, salt caves, time with friends and family . . . I had the capacity for self-care, and I was using it to feed my Soul. I was fragile, raw, and, best of all, willing. I spent the entire year learning to trust my gut and following what felt natural to me. I attended my first-ever weekend retreat, and then my second. I was finding comfort in the moon and began working with her phases. Heads up, if you are a womxn in any kind of business (or not yet following your path), working with the phases of the moon is an INCREDIBLE tool to align the ebbs and flows of goal setting, rest and relaxation, celebration, and release!

The element of my journey that truly changed me was the beautiful healing energy of reiki. I attended weekly intuitive reiki sessions and never left short of amazed. I learned to lean in and understand the somatic symptoms of my body, including the goosebumps. I cultivated a trusting relationship with my own innate wisdom and intuitive gifts. My soul was sparked, a feeling I forever crave to experience as much as possible. I had finally given myself permission to centre in to the natural ebbs and flows of universal alignment, and I was awakening to the magic I had sleeping within me the entire time.

Tokens of Truth

Not everyone will understand you, and it's not important that they do. As your vibration rises, your group will get smaller. Allow it to. Create a cocoon of safety and use discernment around who you allow in it.

Alignment is not your responsibility. Only the Universe can provide it. **You are simply asked to create space** for it. When you are asked to wait, wait. When things are crumbling, let them.

Witness the Prostitute archetype within you. Caroline Myss reminds us that "becoming conscious of how you negotiate your power to find security is crucial to your health. . . .This archetype has you selling out in the shadow, but it can also help you move into an authentic sense of worthiness in the light."[1]

Let your goosebumps be your guide. If you are questioning your truest purpose, cultivate curiosity around the signs you are being shown. Follow what feels light and bright and surround yourself with the things that give you goosebumps.

2019

For the first quarter of the year, I sat with deep fear. I was discovering all these beautiful, magical pieces of myself, and I was feeling the pressure to get back to work. April 1 was approaching quickly—one year of long-term disability leave. I had it all planned out: I would go back part time in an administrative capacity, and I would use the rest of the time to continue exploring the callings of my soul. It made logical sense. It checked all the boxes. Not surprisingly, something was unsettled, and I was full of fear.

Rebecca Campbell, bestselling author of *Light Is the New Black*, tells us that "our highest calling and greatest gift is often tightly nestled right behind our core fear. The higher your calling, the more fear you may have around it."[2] I had casually entertained the idea of sharing my gifts openly with other womxn. I received training in reiki and offered sessions here and there. I had hosted a few small womxn's circles and absolutely loved them. I had started writing again and always dreamed of being a published author. But these didn't fall into the narrative of what a "successful" career would look like, especially when that meant five years of schooling going to waste. What seemed more logical was heading back to work part time and remaining casual with the rest. I would half lean, like a drunken teenager, toward everything my heart and soul desired. But I wasn't ready to take the leap.

Every ounce of my soul was afraid. Every cell in my body told me that to stay safe I should only follow my dreams halfway so I couldn't fail. Every fibre in my being was trying desperately to keep me small and unseen. And here I was, blissfully unaware that the Universe had other plans, and that I was heavily being guided toward being a full-time entrepreneur.

Ultimately, it didn't matter how much I worried about returning to work or fulfilling my duties as a university grad. When I woke up out of a deep sleep and was guided toward creating a business page, I surrendered. I used the name of the blog I had created to share my journey. I had zero expectations of what would come of it, but I was hyperaware of my physical reaction when I was going to push "Publish." It took a lot of effort not to throw up.

This is when something truly shifted for me. When I was able to recognize this intensely nervous and fearful feeling as my soul and my ego colliding, I realized I had a choice. I could radiate, or I could drain. I could survive, or I could thrive. I could choose to let this fear control me, or I could use it as a catalyst to transform me. I could use it as a teacher. And I could learn to trust the Universe to create alignment in all aspects of my life.

This internal shift caused several outward shifts, almost immediately.

A week before April 1, I finished my Usui Holy Fire III Reiki Master Training. The next day I received a call from HR at work saying that I wasn't able to return because they didn't receive the paperwork from my doctor or my long-term disability (LTD) caseworker. I called to speak with my caseworker and was notified that I no longer had a file. It had been bounced around between a couple of workers, and in the process, I had been asked to sign paperwork that closed my file too early. Long-term disability refused to speak to my doctor, who refused to speak to my work, who required information from LTD, in which I no longer had a file. Simply put, the Universe literally made it so that I COULD NOT return to work. And I chose not to fight it. Later that day my mom sent me a screenshot of a holistic health centre looking for a reiki practitioner. The literal moment that space was created in my life, i.e., the moment I was forced to release a job that left me burned out and unfulfilled (and was no longer in alignment with me), something that was aligned with my soul fell right into place.

It happened with relationships too. Following my reiki master training, I had finally settled into the awareness that the relationship I was in was not resonating with this magical, divine love I had witnessed with my grandparents. As scared as I was to lose this person who had such a deep impact in my healing journey, I knew it was an important step to let it go and to create space. On April 1, I was sitting across from Ashley. In that quick moment (that would have been meaningless to everyone else), I felt IT. The IT that everyone craves. The IT that people question whether truly exists. The IT that my grandparents shared. Everything about this beautiful human called to me. I had created space, and my soul mate—my teacher, my challenger, my cheerleader, my best friend—dropped right into my lap. Several friendships ended this year, most without any explanation. And I met the most wonderful people afterward. People who I know in my heart will always be here. People who are connected to my soul, who are part of my family.

Within one week my ENTIRE life had changed, and in that moment, I realized I was meant to leap. Impulsively, fearlessly, with complete trust in the Universe.

What I once imagined for April 2019 was disturbingly inaccurate. Instead, I had officially launched my own business with a rebrand. I had met my sacred soul mate. I was incredibly confident in my reiki practice. I was channelling workshops and events that made an impact and were exciting. I was living the life I had NEVER dreamed of, the life that I was meant to be living. I took a strong step back from micromanaging and was astonished by how the Universe thanked me. I attended The Great Canadian Woman Summit later that year and committed to my goal of becoming a published author. I also hosted two full weekend retreats and married the love of my life. The year 2019 absolutely blew my mind. *Cool note:* It is 4:44 p.m. and our wedding song just started playing. You can't make up this shit!

Tokens of Truth

Life isn't perfect when you choose to fall into alignment. You are challenged to GROW, to question your intentions, to live consciously and full of awareness. You are guided to be kind, understanding, compassionate, and incredibly sensitive.

Take the leap! Trust your journey. It's bigger than you. We are all here to bring our authentic light into this world. There is a business / an occupation / a role that is aligned with you, and it is ALWAYS calling you in its direction. Create space to listen.

The plans that you create for yourself—those are the short straw. Dream those dreams and then release them into the Universe.

When something isn't aligned in your life, and this includes in your business, it will not work. It will teach you a lesson, and if you aren't willing to listen, it will come again and again and again until you do. Trust it the first time.

2020

In December 2019 I was guided to shift my business and allow it to take up space in an online platform, another rebrand. January was the start of this "new" (or rather "different") adventure. It was also my first $20,000 month. I didn't fully embrace the new model, as I continued scheduling in-person trainings and retreats; however, I was guided to schedule most of these for later in the year. I didn't know why, but I'm certainly grateful that I did. I'm grateful that I put my trust in those little nudges the Universe sent my way. Not even two months later the COVID-19 pandemic eliminated all in-person offerings, closed small businesses all over the world, and created fear and instability in almost every household.

The year 2019 had left such a magical impression in my mind that I half expected / really wanted everything to feel that way forever . . . or at least for a really long time. But as is life, we are ebbing and flowing, and we can't enjoy the high tides without having droughts.

I moved into a new home and moved out four months later after having discovered toxic mould and shrews (so gross). Thankfully, due to COVID-19, I was unable to have clients in this home. A new house fell into our laps the second we released control. This house met all our needs and more, and in July I was guided for the fourth time to rebrand and FINALLY stepped into my full power as a spiritual teacher and mentor. I welcomed clients back into my space, and it felt like magic. The fear, discomfort, and change that came with COVID-19 also shifted A LOT of womxn into a space of awakening. And the beauty of it is that it has shifted us toward one another. It shifted us inward. As a collective, I'm sure most of us couldn't wrap our heads around why. And for me, this time was different because I didn't try to. I felt safe in the unknown, and I could hold space for people who were struggling.

Today, I embrace the name The Reiki Witch. It sends shivers of excitement and memory through my cells every time I express it. Goosebumps everywhere. I am in love with the role I keep as a reiki teacher and mentor, in person and online. I see the impact my work has on others every single day, and I KNOW that I am in alignment. That is the true beauty in entrepreneurship: YOU get to choose how you express yourself, and you can choose to allow the Universe to guide you into your unique light. As you continue to heal and expand, so does your business. And in doing so, the people who are connected to YOUR light will come. The magic is always being woven without our knowledge. Although we cannot fathom how the outcome can be best for us, if we allow the Universe to show us, we won't be disappointed!

A Final Token of Truth

You are being aligned faster than most because you are open and aware. You have taken the steps you've been asked to take, to have willingness, to surrender, to expand. There is a huge reason that you are being entrusted with the Universe's plan to align the collective. You are a leader. You are here to tread the difficult terrain and clear the path for others. You are being asked to move the sticks and stones, fumble on the obstacles, and create new pathways for future generations. You are being asked and guided to find your true centre, create space for your true alignment, expand your true self, and settle deeply into that space within you. And no, that's not easy . . . that's a massive journey in and of itself. And you aren't done. Then you are guided to inspire others to come and join you, no matter what that looks like for them. We are all being guided toward different careers, businesses, opportunities, lessons, relationships . . . and this is especially why there is no room for comparison or competition. Each of our respective journeys are bringing us to the greater space of Source Alignment, of Love, of Compassion, of Courage, of Truth. Please, embrace YOUR journey. This, I'm guided to share, is your ONLY job. Drop the agenda your Ego carries and completely surrender, creating conscious harmony with the Universe, in all aspects of your life. To dismiss this is to do a grave disservice to the beautiful world in which you've been asked to cultivate your true and authentic life.

Lindsay Anderson

Lindsay Anderson is a personal-development junkie. She's a moon-loving, sushi-addicted spiritual badass who shines her light unapologetically in all that she does. She lives in her truth and doesn't shy away from the discomfort of deep healing. Lindsay is the owner of The Reiki Witch in Ontario, Canada, where she helps other womxn awaken to the magic within. She is a Usui/Holy Fire III Reiki Master Teacher and spiritual-development mentor. Lindsay has a bachelor's degree with honours in Social Work and a Social Service Worker diploma, which lend to her ability to hold brave, safe, and sacred space for those around her. After graduating in 2015, Lindsay worked in the field of mental health before suffering from vicarious trauma and burnout. Her rock bottom created space for her awakening. Over the last two years, she has embraced her empathic and intuitive abilities and has trusted the Universe to guide her life. In that time, she has married her soul mate, become a published author, and started a very successful spiritual business. Her offerings have been described as "nothing short of soul shaking." Lindsay keeps it real, smashing the comfort zones that have kept her small and revealing her authentic self, little by little, every single day. If you're part of this girl's circle, you know you're going to be inspired!

🌐 www.thereikiwitch.ca

📷 @the.reikiwitch

f the.reikiwitch

My family, thank you for your unwavering support and unconditional love, especially when I make it hard! Ashley, my supercool wife . . . thank you for always encouraging my dreams. Jen, thank you for being messy with me. I couldn't do this life without any of you.

Emma-Bean and the rest of my Soul Sisters (you know who you are): Thank you for honouring your soul's calling and stepping into my life. Thank you for showing up and embracing your healing and awakening and thank you for allowing me to be a small part of your stories.

She Is

Resilient

CHAPTER 6

FROM CHILD TO CERTIFIED TO COACH

Emily Murcar

As I walked across the stage at our Spring Convocation '14 to accept my diploma in Child Life Studies, I had absolutely no inclination that I would soon be the one wearing diapers! That following September, I was involved in a motor vehicle accident after volunteering at McMaster Children's Hospital and was admitted to the nearest ICU with catastrophic injuries. In a twist of fate, I was now the dependent patient with a childlike innocence, comparable to those I had been supporting that very afternoon! Along with an extended rehabilitation, this experience handed me the surreal opportunity to even further understand the brains of the little people I work with by returning to childhood.

I felt incredibly fortunate to be accepted into McMaster's renowned program with a small, ambitious group of others, all with the same intention of becoming a Certified Child Life Specialist (CCLS). I can recall explaining to my guidance counsellor in high school that I wanted to "work with children and mental health," and Child Life appeared to be a career that was created just for me. Coming with a wide range of experiences and credentials, my group would come to be considered the experts in child development, a vital addition to the paediatric health care team and the "voice of the child" when they could not speak for themselves. Our convocation rewarded me with what was supposed to be my final educational accomplishment: specializing in an understanding of the developmental needs of children and youth, newborn through adolescence—physically, emotionally, and psychosocially.

> *"Do you ever look at someone and wonder*
> *what is going on inside their head?"* — Joy

The film *Inside Out* begins with a screaming introduction to the main character in a hospital, fittingly enough. Released in June 2015, this Pixar movie provided me with a visual to understand what had been occurring inside my own head. For example, the introductory glimpse into young Riley's brain includes the construction of her "control centre" at birth and her five core emotions beginning with **Joy**, followed immediately by **Sadness**, and eventually, **Disgust**, **Anger**, and **Fear**. The five main emotions are in constant interaction with each other, navigating Riley's behaviour and decisions throughout her childhood. I could relate because the crash had made an impact on my busy and bustling life and even simple day-to-day decisions! The film illustrates a new awareness of my own brain.

Child Life Specialists (CLS) empower the patients they work intimately with to express their emotions and learn ways to help themselves cope through various interventions. With this encouragement, children can rehearse verbalizing their feelings of **Sadness** to others and participate in any legacy-building or memory-making activities. The CLS will create familiarity with the procedures, diagnoses, and medicines through medical play, giving **Fear** a focus, while further exploring the child's dislikes. Teaching patients about the stinky and undesirable aspects of their own medical care, while allowing them to participate in their decision-making (whenever possible) allows **Disgust's** voice to be acknowledged. Relaxation techniques and other appropriate ways to release their **Anger** are also discussed. Lastly, we cultivate **Joy** in our patients by normalizing the hospital environment to be less threatening, incorporating play whenever possible. Alas, I joked during my entire hospital stay that I needed to hire my own Adult Life Specialist!

* * *

It took the team of paramedics forty-seven minutes to successfully extract me from my Volkswagen Golf; the only part of my car that was intact and accurately placed was the driver's seat. My physical injuries included seven broken ribs, a broken left wrist, and a shattered pelvis that would force me on bedrest for the following three months. Additionally, I had suffered a brain bleed with an undetermined severity of an Acquired Brain Injury (ABI), though I had a positive prognosis. It was communicated to my parents that I was able to decipher between my lefts and rights upon my entry into Emergency despite the fact that half my paperwork coming in from the paramedics prematurely declared my status as "deceased." I was immediately put into a medically induced coma to prevent any further damage.

Speaking of which, it is worth noting that I am often asked whether I recall anything from my *ten* days in a coma. It sounds unbelievable, but I truly believed I was miraculously waking up at my own "funeral wake," and that a vital error must have occurred somewhere along the medical chain! All the evidence playing out before my eyes supported this outrageous thought: I could not scream out those pleas that a grave mistake was being made, I could not move any other part of my body, and I was nestled and resting comfortably in a "casket." Furthermore, the steady flow of "tearful funeral guests" made complete sense; they were a mixture of my past and present!

Because my short-term memory was limited after the crash, I

have been told how I was constantly confused at first, with similar scenes playing out on subsequent mornings. Once I had again grasped what had happened to me, my first two questions were always, "Is everyone else okay?" and "Was it my fault?" My family was told not to worry too much yet. In reflecting now, it is clear that there was no awareness for me of the reality of the situation at that point in time.

I "compromised" with my parents that I would only stay in the hospital for two more nights, but I was absolutely insistent that I was going home for the weekend! Also, I was in complete disbelief when I discovered that my Child Life Certification exam had been rescheduled without my input on the matter. According to my last memories, I had just completed my registration online, and this exam was a culmination of *everything* I had been working toward! I was convinced that everyone was simply overreacting, and I would still be writing it a month later alongside my peers. Likewise, I insisted that my new basement apartment would certainly be feasible upon discharge; I was convinced I was going to work really hard just as I had for everything else I had accomplished in my life! At this point in time I was overly optimistic, and I did not realize the control my brain truly had over my life.

Having three months in a hospital bed to reflect on my life, I easily managed to find the humour in my situation. The irony of this entire ordeal was overwhelming! I was a recently graduated CLS, who had just spent the previous year before the crash supporting families through their own tragedies, and I had just applied to write my certification exam. I had immersed myself into the world of Child Life within various hospital environments, absorbing as much information about children during the formative years and beyond that I possibly could, and I was planning the next steps in my career path. Without any warning, I had been handed a non-negotiable invitation to actually live those developmental stages in an accurate sequence. Consequently, I have now had a five-year rehabilitation period taking priority over *any* goals that I may have dreamed about for the first years of this new decade.

Since my own diagnosis, I have also learned that there are no ABIs exactly the same. Similarly, patients' responses and emotions to hospitalization can vastly differ across stressful situations. A CLS will reason why the child is coping the way they are based on their age, intellectual level, stage of development, past experiences, religion, family structure, and much more. From their first introduction, a CLS determines how the child is responding psychosocially as the impact the environmental factors have on their behaviours are exhibited. Through subsequent visits, the CLS makes ongoing assessments and evaluates how a child is coping, while taking into consideration the individual diagnoses.

"Say what you want; I think it's all
beautiful." — Joy

During my time in the hospital and ABI Clinic, it was extremely clear to those around me and visitors who came that **Joy** was independently dominating. For example, soon after I emerged from my coma, I fuzzily recall my little niece and nephew entering my room for their first time, and they were quite uncomfortable. Sensing their unease and discombobulation in the situation, I chose to make them (and the entire room!) giggle by throwing off my blankets and flashing my diaper as an assurance that I had not changed. Due to an overwhelming sense of gratitude for this second chance at life (and that no others were harmed in the painful process!), my positive and perky disposition easily made friends. Regardless of what had transpired physically on the outside, this attitude illustrated my perspective that I was so incredibly fortunate and had the confidence that everything still felt like "me" on the inside. (*Side note:* Nurses and visiting physicians and other medical staff will *never* forget a face that hand delivers fresh baked goods or salty snacks, especially with a smile!) In addition to exuding pure happiness in every interaction, I was teased by my professional colleagues during their visits for trying "to Child Life the place up as much as possible, everywhere I went!" I even once compared my experience within the ABI Clinic to living in a university residence!

> *"All right! We did not die today; I call that an unqualified success!"* — Fear

I was familiar with the procedures and policies of a health care environment and the expectations of me as a patient within it, which made my **Fear** quite minimal in the beginning. Whereas a child may experience **Fear** at a maximum level when first waking up in the hospital, I suppose I hadn't quite realized the full gravity of my situation. My short stint in the hospital was truly only a taste of the debilitating effects of living with an anxiety disorder. After my transition from the ABI Clinic to home, I was constantly plagued with numerous, horrifying visions of worst-case scenarios playing themselves out in detail in my head. These apparitions were automatically fabricated in everyday, normal situations, but there were a few examples that remain in my memory as persistent and are the hardest to work through.

At the beginning of my recovery, I learned to walk again in a public pool, but I first had to navigate the slippery deck with my walker. I absolutely dreaded getting in and out of the pool and would cling to my physiotherapy assistant. Another hurdle for my brain to battle was the treadmill at the gym that overlooked the gymnasium. My imagination would repeatedly show me diving headfirst through the glass barrier after accidentally hitting the speed button. I thought about this possibility every time I stepped onto that treadmill for more than two years. I had to repeat to myself that the word *fear* itself stood for "*False Evidence Appearing Real*," but self-talk can only take you so far! I silently battled these fantasies until it was confirmed that I had been struggling with symptoms of post-traumatic stress disorder (PTSD). I was told that despite my brain not logging the memory into its long-term library, it was clear that my body remembered what had transpired. For a visual, if you have ever watched the Christmas movie *Elf* with Will Ferrell, you have insight into me attempting to first step onto an escalator at the mall post-accident.

> *"It's the worst place I've been in my entire life."* — Disgust

Of course, **Disgust** enjoyed tagging along with **Fear** in all these situations, especially when I attempted to return to my volunteering position at McMaster Children's Hospital. Perhaps it was because my brain was no longer associating that environment with a place of volunteering or employment, but more so, it was my former living space; it had been my *home* for almost three months! At that time, it was evident that I had limitations I was still learning about and my awareness of these helped me make the difficult decision to put that commitment temporarily behind me. Alternatively, I had continued my volunteering at The Lighthouse Program for Grieving Children as a group facilitator, where I found solace and a newfound sense of gratefulness through peer support.

> *"We could cry until we can't breathe!"* — Sadness

In the next chapter of my journey to recovery there was a constant power struggle between my **Sadness** and **Anger**. Each took turns ruling the roost, with the other always trailing in right behind. These two were partners in crime, and I was the only victim . . . yet again. I cried miserable tears, furious tears, mopey tears, and frustrated tears; there were the type of tears that I would shamefully hide behind my sunglasses and others that were free flowing and uncontrolled, directly alongside my behaviour. **Fear** had primarily stepped into the background, but it would make a reappearance as my uninvited date for social events or group settings. I was always unsure of what would escape past my filters. This fear also affected my ability to keep in touch with most of my friends and family as I would only talk on the phone with *very* few people.

From the beginning, I have wanted to look at an ABI growth chart to measure my progress since the crash and be convinced that I am one hundred percent where I should be. It has been even more maddening to not be able to determine the expectations for any level! There was no constructive feedback on how I could do better for the next evaluation! Instead, with much coaching, I have trained myself to stop making comparisons across the ABI population. As mentioned, the symptoms and recovery with an ABI are different for each survivor, much like as in people with multiple sclerosis or even a snowflake. In fact, my esteemed neuropsychologist reassured me by saying, "You are exactly where you are supposed to be," and I remind myself and others of this statement on a regular basis.

"Can I say that curse word now?" — **Anger**

Furthermore, if there is one aspect of my journey that is imperative in understanding the consequences of the crash on my life, it would be that it has classified me as a survivor . . . an Acquired Brain Injury survivor. As much as this experience has affected the current chapter of my life, its diagnosis also carries lifelong implications of having an "invisible illness." Honestly, my physical injuries do not even compare to the consequences that an ABI places upon my life, despite maximum efforts from all parties involved. It is not uncommon for me to share that I would have traded fracturing all 206 bones in my body if my brain had been kept safe from harm. The extra factor of the brain injury complicates multi-tasking and distractibility in every situation, which even includes completing more than two tasks simultaneously in the kitchen or trying to hold your bladder through a conversation (much to my surprise!). Essentially, any action that humans perform automatically without a second thought requires a step-by-step instruction manual from the injured computer upon the ABI survivor's shoulders! Walking is no longer an uncomplicated task, especially either up or down a flight of stairs while having a conversation or carrying more than one object per hand or even attempting to adjust one's ponytail. The paradox of having an unofficial diagnosis of obsessive-compulsive disorder, combined with a type A personality allows for my never-ending lists and box checking to now just be a necessary part of my daily routines.

My warm-hearted physiotherapist and I made a goal to have me riding a bicycle by the end of summer 2016, but that possibility became less and less likely with my own stress, anxieties, balance issues, and again, the **Fear** resurfacing. I have a hunch that he would speak not only to my overreaching and unrealistic goals but also to my determination and fierce passion in achieving them. I am also confident that he could further speak to my unique, emotional roller coaster since our first encounter in my hospital room to a daily, then weekly regime. This influential individual is extremely familiar with his clients arriving to frequent appointments in tears, angry outbursts, excruciating pain, or in need of a supportive and motivating pep talk.

> *"Sadness. Mom and Dad, the team . . . they came to help because of Sadness."* — Joy

Much like Riley in *Inside Out*, I learned a deeper appreciation for the **Sadness** in my life because it assisted me in enhancing and truly rediscovering my own **Joy**. Moreover, I also had a team come lift me when I couldn't get up myself. Leaning into my **Sadness** allowed me to strengthen my own resilience and live an intentional rehabilitation, fiercely pursuing the goals from five years before that still applied to my "new normal." To illustrate, almost a year to the date I was originally supposed to take the Child Life Certification exam, I passed it. To outsiders, I may appear like the same individual on the outside, but the hand of cards I have been dealt this round have certainly challenged me . . . and changed me like I *never* could have even imagined. I constantly remind myself that I definitely despise being the three-year-old having an inconsolable meltdown about not getting her own way and the awkward seventeen-year-old struggling with communication. But the most important aspect that I have finally acknowledged is that I am *still* Emily—a successful, accomplished, working, sociable, bubbly, and busy (finally!) thirty-six-year-old.

More importantly, this event has painted a perfect picture of how a successful and collaborative health care team should function. The members of my interdisciplinary team all have differing levels of knowledge, education, professional skills, and personalities, but all have the commonality of working intimately with patients with brain injuries of all ages. Each of these extraordinary individuals have assisted me in reinventing the new version of myself, a "new normal" to navigate through this next unplanned stage of my life.

However, above all, my professional experiences have perfectly prepared me for being a patient in a sense, both a hospitalized one and within the community. This experience allowed me to even further understand the child's perspective and what we should consider during stressful situations (even the little things!), especially with children or teens who are conflicted, frightened, or confused. This understanding certainly extends to include the needs of the family as well, especially siblings! Perhaps having the knowledge, images, visualizations, and memory of everything I've learned *before*, but the inability to effectively communicate them *after*, has been the most insufferable transition throughout my recovery. Nevertheless, I will continue to wear my newfound appreciation for life like a badge of honour. I am confident that my experience will help the children of the future—mine, yours, and everyone's—cultivate their own gratitude for life and love for themselves. I want to continue to engage with families as a whole in the continued search of the eternal inner child that each of us possess within.

Emily Murcar

Raised in Burlington, Ontario, Emily Murcar is an only child and was a fiery July baby. From a young age, Emily has enjoyed children, animals, and friendships—she has been a "social butterfly" from the start! Following high school, Emily graduated from Wilfrid Laurier University (Honours BA, Psychology and Sociology) and Queen's University (BEd, Primary/Junior). When a friend opened her eyes to the wonderful world of Child Life, Emily graduated from McMaster University having stumbled upon the career that was undoubtedly created for her.

"How we walk with the broken speaks louder than how we sit with the great." - Ben Bennot

Emily has always been empathetic and committed to the mental health of children and youth, especially among the tiniest population! Her career interests lie within gender diversity, grief and bereavement, and trauma and transitions. Presently, Emily is studying at the Centre of Applied Neuroscience (Toronto) to become a Certified Life Coach, learning about her own brain and those of the children and youth with whom she works. Emily envisions establishing her vision of Child Life Coaching, a safe space where children are encouraged to explore their feelings, set achievable goals, and become empowered to live their best lives. When not dedicating her time to the welfare of youth, extraordinary Emily leads an ordinary life of (frugal) shopping, socializing with family and friends, scrapbooking, or "coaching" her Bernese Mountain dog puppy, Cola.

Firstly, thank you to our own great Canadian woman, Sarah Swain, and the rest of her team for both the opportunity to share my story with the world and their infinite patience with me.

Of course, it goes without question that my rehabilitation team, including my legal duo, were a committed group of individuals and a vital part of my recovery. Thank you with the deepest sense of gratitude for assisting me in embracing my new normal. The support you provided was unwavering and sincere.

Lastly, and most importantly, I express my thanks to my family and friends who loved the "before" me and still love the "after" me, especially my compassionate parents. Though I was not quite prepared for this type of storm, you are each a part of my rainbow that follows it.

She Is

Honest

CHAPTER 7

THE GOOD, THE BAD, AND THE UNFAITHFUL: HOW I LIVED THROUGH MY DIVORCE

Erin Montgomery

Welcome to my pity party.

The curtains are drawn, the wine is free flowing, and the tears just never stop. To the right you will find an enormous pile of crumpled up laundry, to the left an overflowing sink of unwashed dishes, and over in the back sits my self-worth and, for lack of a better term, my happiness.

Dress code for this event? All the sweatpants and oversized hoodies. Oh, you like my smoky eye? That is thanks to three days of unwashed mascara patted down with caked-on foundation. Pretty, right?

Divorce. It hits you like a ton of bricks at the most unsuspecting time. It's like a tidal wave that doesn't ever slow down, engrossing you in an unimaginable number of waves you just can't seem to escape. No matter how hard you try and swim or how many times you gasp for air, it's like you're drowning—drowning in the memories of what once was and of what's to come.

Divorce is like this taboo subject no one wants to talk about, no one wants to associate themselves with, and absolutely no one ever thinks will happen to them. Well, NEWS FLASH: Divorce is real. It happens WAY more than you think, and I can promise you that it's not contagious.

When I stood in front of a room filled with my family and friends and said I do (only hesitating slightly), I wasn't expecting to be announcing a divorce just eight short years later. Did I get married too young? Absolutely. Did I perhaps get married for the wrong reasons? Probably. Did I get married with the intention of getting a divorce? Absolutely not!

But here I am—a thirty-four-year-old divorced single mama of three. Treading water every day, just turning to keep my head up.

I can still remember the day he told me he wanted a divorce. It's one of those memories engraved into my head that I am certain I will never be able to forget. It wasn't a particularly memorable day; we weren't fighting or playing the silent game with each other, we were just sitting in our family room. We were probably watching the hundredth episode of *Paw Patrol* with our three children on the couch, one of whom was just four months old.

I had just celebrated my thirty-second birthday. It was late August, it was hot, and I remember how calm he was when he spoke. All he said was "What would you say if I told you I wanted to separate?"

Separate? That idea hadn't even crossed my mind. We had children. We had a house, a mortgage, credit card debt. Separation was the last thing that I was thinking about. How could he even ask me that? What had I done for him to think that separation was a good idea? He couldn't be serious, could he?

My mind was whirling with a million different questions. What? Why? When? How? Whose idea was this? There is no way he would have come up with this idea on his own. I gave him everything: all the free time in the world, three children, home-cooked meals, a clean house, E-V-E-R-Y-T-H-I-N-G.

But at that moment, none of those questions came out. I didn't yell or cry or fight him. I simply said, "I would say no!" And that was that. The conversation was over. At least so I thought.

At this specific point in our marriage, we had just celebrated our eighth anniversary and had just welcomed our third child, our second son. He was just four months old, and my husband was on parental leave while I went back to work. I worked day and night as a bartender. From 10:00 a.m. until 10:00 p.m., I was behind the bar, pouring drinks, chatting up customers, and providing for my family, all while I thought my husband was at home caring for our three children. Well, only part of that was true.

After his initial outburst of the idea of separation, I quickly learned that there was someone else. He met her at our son's karate class. She was a single mom. And he thought he loved her. But of course, he didn't. It was just lust and perhaps a bit of the seven-year-marriage itch. Maybe he thought there was something better out there for him. Maybe he missed the thrill of dating. I'm not entirely sure what he thought. But I knew he didn't think staying with me was the right decision.

The weeks that followed our initial conversation were some of the darkest weeks of my life. He was serious about divorce, and no amount of pleading and promising was going to change his mind. So, I began to accept my fate.

I shut down. I lost weight. I lost interest in everything. I cut myself off from friends. I lost my smile, my voice, and my self-worth. My job hung on by a thread. I was miserable.

And the worst part? I had to come home to him every night.

* * *

Divorce has this funny way of making you forget all the bad things that happened in your marriage. I did not have a perfect marriage, but instead of looking at all the things that would have led us to a divorce, the only thing I could focus on is what I did wrong. I mean, I must have done something to make him want a divorce, right?

WRONG.

If I look back now, I can replay all the moments in our relationship that led up to our divorce. But in that initial moment I somehow couldn't come up with one thing that would make me think we were headed for divorce. We were too young to be married, we got married because I was pregnant, and we had NO IDEA what we were doing. But there was also quite a bit of infidelity on his part. And I overlooked it, each and every time. Because we had kids, because we were married, because I didn't want to disappoint my family by getting a divorce.

But that divorce happened anyway.

As shocked as I was, I think in the back of my head I knew it was going to happen. It was just a matter of time. We had eight years of marriage. Eight years of cheating, eight years of me putting myself last, eight years of debt, eight years of him slowly chipping away at my self-esteem.

Was I sad that he was the one to pull the divorce trigger? Kind of.

I didn't stand up for myself during our marriage. I rolled over and let everything happen. I plastered a smile on my face and pretended everything was fine. From the outside looking in, we appeared like an awesome couple. We never fought, we had three children, we owned a house, we seemed like the picture-perfect family. But no one really knows what goes on behind closed doors. And I never shared the truth.

The truth was, I was unhappy. I was everything I swore I would never be. I gave up who I was for our marriage. I stayed home every day, every night, and every weekend. I let him have his freedom—far too much—I let him call me names and cheat on me. I made excuses for him; I protected and defended him at all costs. I let him live his life, which, in turn, made me forget how to live mine.

*   *   *

We were separated for nearly four months before he finally moved out. I walked on eggshells around him during those four months, careful not to set him off or send him running into the arms of his lover. I think I still held on to this weird hope that maybe this was a phase and that we would fix it. So, I did nothing to stir the pot. I kept quiet. I exchanged only pleasantries with him. And I still did all the laundry and all cooking, secretly hoping he would change his mind.

But he didn't.

Instead, he used those four months to tear down the last bit of self-respect I had. He threw his new relationship in my face, never trying to hide the text messages or date nights with her. He spoke with her on FaceTime while I sat on the opposite side of the couch. He rushed out to see her when I got home from work, he took our kids to play with her at the park, he shared details of their relationship, and I just smiled, never saying anything.

Then, it happened. Just like I had hoped for. He, for a brief second, wanted to make it work. But it was more of a competition than anything. He was still dating her, still living with me, and still deciding who he wanted to be with.

That was when I knew that this marriage was not worth fighting for.

If he truly loved me, if he really wanted to be with me, he would know it. It wouldn't be a competition. I shouldn't have to compete for my own husband. And so, I didn't.

I stopped caring, stopped reacting, stopped trying to prove to him how much I loved him. And he moved out. He moved out in the heat of the moment, at two o'clock in the morning. He threw his clothes in a garbage bag, and he was gone.

But our journey to a positive co-parenting relationship was far from over. After he left, I was in a big house alone, with three children who depended on me immensely. I couldn't afford to pay our mortgage, our property taxes, and our monthly credit card bills. I could barely put food on the table.

I slipped deeper and deeper into self-hatred. Every night I had a pity party for one, and the only invitee was a bottle of wine. I cried so much I think I literally ran out of tears, if that is even possible. I stopped eating, and I stopped showing up in my own life. I spent my days wearing a fake smile for my kids and my nights so engulfed in tears that I never really slept.

But my story doesn't end there.

The feelings of self-hatred and failure didn't last forever. Every day, I cried one less tear and had one less negative thought.

It's been just over two years and I can now say that I have moved past everything that once was. I no longer hold onto any resentment toward him or even the woman for whom he left.

When I was in the thick of my pity parties, I realized that if I didn't get up the next morning and take care of my children, who would? If I didn't figure out a way to pay the bills, who would? If I didn't love myself, who would?

These are the questions that helped me rediscover who I was. It was in those moments that I realized that I was a woman, a mother, and a dreamer, and I deserved the best out of life, regardless if that meant being married or not.

That first year of separation was the most trying time in my life. The number of emotions that I experienced on a daily basis were incredible. But I also learned that divorce isn't something that you have to be labelled with for the rest of your life. We are all in charge of our own destiny. Who we want to be and who we become is all up to us.

Divorce was a life-changing experience. It rocked my world. It took me down a rabbit hole of self-hatred I wouldn't wish on anyone. However, it also taught me resilience. It gave me strength I never knew I had. It showed me that no matter how much life beats you down, there is always something brighter to come.

It's been two years now and I am more in love with my life than

I ever was. I found my groove again. I rediscovered everything that I was passionate about, and I turned that into a self-respecting career that I am incredibly proud of.

Divorce led me down a rocky path with about forty different forks in the road. I experienced emotions that were so encompassing that I didn't think I would ever be able to live again. But now, looking back, I really don't think I would be where I am today without my divorce.

My divorce was part of my journey. It was a necessary step in order for me to find myself again. My divorce will always be a part of my journey. I don't regret it. Most days I don't even think about it. But somewhere in the back of my mind I can acknowledge that my divorce led me to be the woman I am today.

Today, I am a single mom to three children. I am a taxi driver, the lunch lady, the nurse, the cheerleader at every game. But I am also a business owner, an editor, a published author. I created the life I knew I had always wanted. I finally found the courage to follow my dreams.

I made it. Divorce threw a wrench in my perfect little life, but the truth is, it was never really perfect to begin with. I truly believe that we, as women, need to stop painting a portrait of a perfect life that we think everyone wants to see. We need to stop plastering on a fake smile and pretending that our marriage hasn't been through rocky times. We need to share all the trials and tribulations that we have been through. We need to show other

THE GREAT CANADIAN WOMAN

women that they are not alone. We need to find our voices and shout our stories from the rooftops. Together, as women, we can overcome anything. But we need to know that someone else has been in our shoes, has walked that same broken path, and that is exactly why I needed to share this story.

Somewhere, there is another woman who is in the same position I was. A woman whose husband has been unfaithful, a woman who is trying so desperately to hold together that picture of a perfect family that she has painted over the years. A woman who needs to know that there is something brighter waiting for her.

There is something brighter waiting for you. I found it and so will you. Divorce doesn't have to be the end of your story. Divorce is just the beginning.

Erin Montgomery

Erin Montgomery is a journalism graduate with more than ten years of writing experience. Over the years, Erin has developed her skills to include Public Relations, social media advertising and marketing, media relations, and web design. Erin is also the editor and founder of Flourish Magazine, which is a quarterly magazine written for moms, by moms. Flourish is all about real talk, no expert advice. Erin is a single mom to three little ones and resides just outside of Hamilton, Ontario.

@thewriterwithrednails

They say it takes a village to raise children, but that village not only helps raise your children, it also helps raise you up when you fall down. To my village, thank you for your unwavering support. Without the help of my village I wouldn't be where I am today, and this chapter would forever be a work in progress. For everyone who has stood in my corner and to my kids who have taught me resilience and brought me immense strength, thank you. I couldn't have done this without you.

She Is

—— Kind

CHAPTER 8

PERSEVERANCE, KINDNESS, AND BECOMING A GODDAMN WARRIOR

Sarah Vaill-Ciano

I haven't graced this planet for a long time, but I do feel like I have lived many lives. I've had many opportunities to weave in and out of lots of life lessons, and for the most part, I have become victorious. As a child, you never know where your life is going to take you. Some people ride the wave that is pre-planned for them with minimal effort or discomfort. Some of us, however, take the falling down the mountainside, hitting-every-rock-on-the-way-down approach. Both ways get you to the bottom, but with the latter, you end up a little more bruised and broken.

I have always been a big believer in that what you do with that broken mess of yourself is what really makes the difference. I could have picked different paths than I did, but what fun would that have been? Today, I am the person who people look to for advice, a sage of wisdom for my two young children, and the collector of wandering lost souls. I am a mother, wife, friend, witch, master reiki practitioner, plant goddess, lover of the moon, pirate, and speaker of the divine feminine, and I love every part of the Me that I have become.

To say my relationship with spirituality has been a long, tumultuous one would be an understatement. Mom and Dad grew up Catholic but never pushed organized religion on us. We never went to church. I learned the serenity prayer by standing hand in hand with strangers on Friday nights. When I was growing up, my parents were alcoholics. They divorced when I was two, so that was the only family dynamic I had ever known. My mother struggled with addiction through most of my childhood, which caused me to be a bit of a vagabond—staying at friends' houses and finding families that wouldn't kick me out after more than one night. I stayed with families that treated me like one of their own; I bet it felt like I would never leave, but I am so thankful for them. These people saved me and allowed me to see a family model: mom, dad, kids, dog = family.

Believe it or not, I was always a happy kid. I was in leadership programs in school and captain of every team I played on. I could also give Jim Carrey a run for his money with comedic timing. Except for a handful of people, no one knew what my life was. Experience at home left a lot to be desired and would typically result in us looking to my older sister for guidance and direction. We were all pretty self-sufficient; I don't know many nine-year-olds who can construct a whole meal out of flour, water, and a block of cheese.

Without much guidance or really anyone to answer to left a lot up to interpretation for a teenager. Partying, drinking—hell, the sky's the limit when you don't have to answer to anyone. I was a pretty "street-smart" kid; I knew what trouble to play with and what to stay out of, but sometimes life throws you a curveball to keep you on your toes.

One day when I was fifteen, I was home alone with my mom. I had locked myself in my room and was redecorating because that's what I usually did as an angsty teen and how I tried to escape the chaos that was hiding downstairs. My mom, who had been drinking all day, came up to my room a handful of times to ask me to come and hang out and drink or get high if I wanted to, and my standard response to her was "Can you get the fuck out?!"

It was always easier to pretend that the chaos didn't exist then to go down and face it. My room was my safe space. I was able to just go about living the life that I wanted to live in the safety of my room versus the life that tagged along in my real life. Little did I know that day was that my mom was looking for a reason not to go back downstairs and kill herself. I finally came out of my room about thirty minutes after the last time she came up and found her passed out on the couch, beer bottles and pill bottles everywhere. I called 911, and paramedics got to us just in time. That moment changed me forever. Now, when I think back to a little lost girl who sat there scared and crying in the corner of her kitchen alone, my heart breaks. I couldn't get a hold of my sister, my dad, or anyone, and I finally ran into the streets, looking for anyone that could be an adult at that moment. I remember sitting in my kitchen as the paramedics asked me questions about my mom, which I didn't have the answers to. I was just a deep, dark hole of hurt and confusion. No one really knew what to say or how to deal with me. What can you say? I still feel this hurt. I feel it deep down, and it's almost hard to breathe because I can close my eyes and transport myself back to this moment and the pain is as real now as it was then. You get very little help in those moments when the person driving the ship can't help herself, so I stuffed it down deep, put my head down, and tried to forget it.

With my newfound trauma and heartache and stubborn-as-a-mule personality, the party continued (insert tall, green-eyed, twenty-something-year-old). My sister's long-time boyfriend had a best friend, so I had known this friend for years. However, this was the first time he had ever caught my eye. To my sister's dismay and my now-brother-in-law's surprise, I was able to charm the pants off him (literally).

Had I not been seventeen, or if I had listened to my sister and my friends or prayed to the heavens above, I would have never gotten together with him. But I had seen the model of behaviour in families that I wanted, and it was older dad, younger mom. BOOM happily ever after.

We continued to party because he had a car and a good job, and I had a fake ID. It was pretty much a recipe for disaster or a blessing and curse depending on who you asked that day. I got pregnant and decided that I wanted to be a "real mom." So with the support of my then-husband, we got a place together and played house, but shit got real faster than my overzealous, misguided, headstrong teenage self could have ever imagined. The one thing that kept me going despite not knowing what the sweet shit I was doing was that I now had a reason. My daughter.

As I held my beautiful little girl, the realization that someone had tried to give up on us came to the forefront of my mind. I was never going to give up on my daughter like others had given up on me. My children have been my reason for everything since they came along. They are what get me out of bed, keep my depression from eating me whole, and they even loved me in my exhausted and working-three-jobs state. They light my soul the way nothing else can.

IT WAS TIME TO GET REAL.

My then-husband and I rented an apartment under an older couple's home, and I immediately fell in love with the older woman. She was everything I wanted in a mom. She taught me to sew and bake, she watched *Wheel of Fortune*, and she agreed to watch my daughter at four months old so I could return to school as a full-time college student and graduate with honours in Business.

That's when all the fun started. Just when I thought I had it all together, the universe had a new way of testing me. The years that followed showed me everything I could be and what I definitely couldn't be. We lived a white-picket-fence life—great jobs, beautiful kids, a trailer, dirt bikes, etc. But unfortunately, you can only live the fabulous Facebook lie for so long.

My husband was unfaithful through most of our marriage, which made my twenty-something-year-old mind spin. Was I not good enough? What more could I do? Mother, wife, full-time employee. I had put up with lots of emotional cheating and full-on affairs and then he decided to come home one day and tell me he was leaving me. At the end of it all, our marriage crumbled in betrayal, deception, and lies. I felt like I was being swallowed whole. I was transported back to my kitchen, where that scared fifteen-year-old lost her security and safety, piece by piece. I couldn't cry; I could barely breathe. I remember trying to leave. I even got my own place and moved out with my babies to get away from the dishonesty and hurt. Then, we decided to work it out and make it better for our little family, but all it did was prolong the hurt. It took a couple of days of him leaving to go to his new girlfriend's house and us knowing where he was going to really hit home.

Until then, I don't think that I had ever prayed; I only knew the serenity prayer, but I didn't have much faith in it, to be very honest. I got into my car, and it was freezing. I only had a T-shirt on, and I remember screaming at the top of my lungs, "If there is somebody out there, if somebody is watching me and taking care of me, help me. Please, please, please help me because I don't know what the fuck I am going to do." I begged because I was twenty-five with two kids and married for five years. We had been together for seven years, I had a full-time career, and I was a homeowner. I had lived a life that lots of people don't get to live, let alone at twenty-five, and I was still at a complete loss as to what I was even going to do. That night I crawled into bed alone and cried until my face hurt. I fell into the deepest sleep I had had in almost my whole life. I woke up to what sounded like my door opening and the feeling of a person on the bed. It was like somebody had sat down and put their hand on my foot. At first, I thought it was my husband, and my initial reaction was to kick him right in the face. But suddenly a very calm sensation came over me and then I kind of got scared. Should I look and see who was at the end of my bed? I took the five-year-old approach, brought the blanket up around my head and peeked over my shoulder, only to find nothing there. No one. I just laid there for what felt like all night. I must have fallen asleep because I woke up the next morning with a plan. Start to finish. And it all worked. So, pray! That shit is the real deal.

After a couple of days of hiding at friends' houses and crying on my sister's couch, I dusted off my pride, picked up my shit, and got my plan started!

Get a place. Check.

Go back to school. Check.

Exercise. Check.

Be the best fucking mom to my kids! Check.

Do what any respectable adult does when dividing assets—sit wine-drunk across from your ex-partner and Rock Paper Scissors for each belonging in your house like you have never Rock Paper Scissors for a damn thing in your life. Check!

My mom, at this point, had been clean and sober for five years. I'm sure that she was probably terrified to see her youngest daughter's picture-perfect life fall apart. My relationship with my mother was a little tense, but in the years that followed, I got to know her. I got to understand the hurt, fear, and trauma that haunted my mom every day until it became too much. I finally got to see my mom for the kick-ass warrior she was and is. I understand now that she didn't have the resources she needed and was doing the best she could. She taught me that even in adversity and hatred, one should choose kindness. Even when she had nothing, my mom always tried to help mothers and children in similar situations. She would give someone the shirt off her back if it helped them.

Being kind let me be the best co-parent on the planet when doing that seemed impossible. Unfortunately, my ex struggled with some real-life stuff years after we separated. My ex's demons found him, and to this day, the circumstances surrounding that situation break my heart and terrify me. But always choosing kindness allows me to be compassionate when I need to be there for him and my kids. It gives me the ability to step back and see my divorce as a gift. I got married in my twenties, and it might not have been an ideal situation at the time. We were both young, and honestly, we were just two people living out past traumas and trying to change the past. After my divorce, I faced (and am still facing) my darkness. I had to learn to own my part and see how I didn't show up as a present and healthy partner during our years together. I learned so much about myself, and I am eternally grateful that now, with his new wife and two girls, our life is pretty amazing. We are that big, crazy, blended family, and I love every minute.

NEW BEGINNINGS

Being a single mom is not for the faint of heart, let me tell you. I remember that I got the flu during my first month alone, and I realized just how alone I was. I muscled through the morning with my kids, then went to work because I didn't have the option of taking a sick day. I picked up the kids from daycare, got them dinner, did the whole night routine, and got them to sleep. Finally, I was able to have my moment. I ran a bath, and in my fever-ridden state, I climbed in and cried that cry that you feel in your toes. Of all the memories I have of this time in my life, this one sticks like a hot poker. It was then that I promised myself that if I dated again, I would be so picky and so sure of that person I would love that I would know on the cellular level that I would never feel that alone again. The things I cherish about being a single mom are the other women I got to know or that my bond strengthened. The saying "It takes a village" isn't just for raising kids: it's for that mom in the grocery store whose kid is screaming that he wants candy, and she is struggling with the words because it's candy or bread that week; it's for that mom who isn't sure how she is going to fit twenty-eight hours of stuff into one day and somehow be presentable to the outside world, so people don't judge her and think she is a bad mom; it's for that mom who works her full-time job and works two other jobs when her kids go to their dad's on the weekend so getting that treat for the kids isn't a question. I have the most incredible girl gang. I have a total wolf pack. If you ever need help getting through life, assemble a wolf pack of women who have fought their own battles with experience and still have a smile on their faces. These women are the safety net that caught me when I stumbled. They are the women who can dance the night away like no other twenty-something-year-old and then get up and handle business like the boss babe she is at 6:00 the next morning. I don't know how I would have gotten through the crazy, messy life that is mine without these women.

FINDING LOVE AND WALKING INTO MY HIGHER PURPOSE

I want to say that finding my "happily ever after" happened easily. It did not because I am human; I come with my trauma and fears. I come with resistance and misunderstanding. I look out for not only myself but for my children. I am determined to be cautious and not just let anyone ruin my life. Enter Francesco. He has lived a life where he completes his inner work on an hourly/daily/weekly basis. He is the kind of man who prays before dinner, thanks god each day for his blessings, and calls his mama just to chat. He has taught me that having a strong belief in something more than myself is safe, and not just what he believes in, but all faiths. He doesn't care what people think; he is just happy that people have something in their lives and would never lift his eyebrow at it.

Francesco has allowed me to be safe and secure in the person that I am—not work/school Sarah or meeting/sales-pitch Sarah. I mean, deep down roots—sage-burning, tarot-card-reading, dancing-under-the-full-moon ME, and he doesn't so much as bat an eye. He fosters my hopes and dreams into a bigger, better reality than even I could have imagined. I am thankful for that kind of love, and I was ready for it. With this constant support, I was finally able to acknowledge and love my inner child and see where all her pain and insecurities were coming from. With his kind and understanding nature, my life bloomed into something that I could never have imagined.

I have done a ton of work in our seven years together, and not just professionally, but personally. Along this journey, I have become a total "plant mom." When I was growing up, my dad always had a lot of plants; he had an appreciation that I didn't understand at that time. I had three plants given to me when the kids and I moved into our house on the hill. I struggled to keep those things alive; I am pretty sure they died a hundred times and magically came back to life when I realized that I had been neglecting them so severely.

When I moved in with Francesco, I brought those plants with me. As I worked through my past and started seeing what my future looked like, my plants grew with very little attention. Then I realized that plants are a perfect representation of a growing relationship. Plant the seeds of hope and trust. Care and nourish them with love, attention, and communication, then watch how they flourish and change the space they fill. Today, I have more than one hundred indoor plants, and in the summer, I have an organic veggie garden. Around plants, I feel peace. I now appreciate my father's love of plants, and I encourage anyone who is looking for love to love many plants first. They will teach you a thing or two about persistence, love, and patience.

There is a saying that "pressure makes the diamond." Well, my friend, I believe that one million percent! Every time I felt I was under pressure, I got stronger from the inside out. In each experience, I created a new level of strength, courage, and dedication in all aspects of my life. Each time I came out more durable and more resilient—shinier. I genuinely believe that the situations we face in life allow us to come out a little bit more polished, and it's our job to share that shit.

My hope for whoever reads this chapter is that you will know you are outstanding and that you are a goddess having a human experience. So whatever that is, regardless of your skills or whatever happens in the future, know that you can't truly appreciate the light without the dark, that kindness and compassion are superhero qualities, that when in doubt buy a plant, and that all your experiences up until this point make you a GODDAMN warrior. Brené Brown put it best: "You either walk inside your story and own your truth, or you live outside of your story, hustling for your worthiness."[1] It's time to rise up and stand tall.

I want you all to find your pulse. Got it?! Feel it? Our hearts are beating as one. We are all in this together; you are never alone. Give yourself and the people around you a little grace because you never know what's going on with them and vice versa.

Sarah Vaill-Ciano

Sarah Vaill-Ciano is a charismatic wife, mother of two, and rad pet mom whose contagious energy is a total force with which to be reckoned! While taking a path well-travelled by many, from uncertain childhood to young motherhood to soul-crushing divorce, she found herself at a crossroads. "Let my experiences define me or let them align me." Sarah made the decision to let her experiences fuel her intuitive, compassionate, and authentic way of life. For years, she has served as a helpful role model to those seeking inspiration, help, or advice. In 2018 she finally decided to own that role and be intentional about it. Sarah is a Holy Fire III Master Reiki Practitioner, plant mom, and serial entrepreneur. With her determination, quick wit, and passionate soul, she has let very little stand in her way of bringing to life her aligned-over-hustle way of living. Hand in hand with her family and her incredible sisterhood, she has launched her business, Woke Wellness, as her outlet for both personal growth and a safe space for all to join, connect, heal, and align!

@wokewellness.healing

@sarahelizabeth.vc

Francesco, more than words.

Isabelle and Ethan, you are the greatest gift any mother could hope and dream for.

My family, there is no me without you.

She Is

Courageous

CHAPTER 9

TAKING BACK MY LIFE

Jessica Danford

I'm Jess, and I run a virtual wellness community, all while being the primary caregiver for my partner's dad, Andy. If you told me ten years ago that this is what I would be doing with my life, I wouldn't have believed it. After years of depression, anxiety, self-medicating, drug use, and mysterious autoimmune symptoms, I am at a place in my personal journey where I feel empowered to own my story and share more of it. I want to inspire anyone who has similar experiences or may be going through a hard season of life to know you can create a life you love. I had to forgive myself and own my choices to break free of shame, guilt, and anger in order to build myself a life I love, enjoy, and can be proud of. I can look back on my life and see every moment and every life choice that brought me here today, thriving and creating a life I love.

In 2015 I was diagnosed with celiac disease. For most, this diagnosis is devastating news. For me, it was a diagnosis that I clung to and used to propel me into a healthier lifestyle. I spent too many years trying to convince my doctor something was not right with me. They needed to figure out what was causing all my random and seemingly unrelated medical problems. I had to advocate to even be tested for celiac. Despite my presentations of research and pleas for testing, my doctor refused to test me because it is so "rare." Eventually, I had a blood test, which unfortunately came back negative. A false-negative result can happen if you have removed gluten from your diet before being tested. Several years after my "false-negative" test, my younger sister became violently ill and was hospitalized for a short time. The doctor diagnosed her with ulcerative colitis and celiac disease—a genetic autoimmune condition. When they told her, she sort of laughed. They told her it was a very serious illness and not funny, and that she would have to remove gluten from her diet for the rest of her life. She told them she was laughing because her older sister had been saying for years that she had celiac disease, and no one would believe her. Within a month, I was booked for a colonoscopy and endoscopy where it was confirmed I had celiac disease.

In my online forums I share a lot about my current life and journey, but not everything! Social media contains fractional stories, and there is more to me and my *seemingly* "perfect life" than is seen on my current feed. When I opened my direct messages one day and saw a message that said, "Must be nice; I wish I was you with your perfect life," I was angry at first because this person, someone I considered a friend and had met in the online community, had no idea what I had been through or how hard I have struggled and worked to get to where I am now. With that anger came a realization that because I was not revealing some of the hardest parts of my story, I was not being fully authentic; thus, people were comparing themselves to a partial version of me. I immediately felt compelled to share some of the hard stuff that shaped me into the person I am and am still becoming.

When I was diagnosed with celiac, I already knew I had to make lifestyle changes. Previously, I worked hard, partied harder, was always on the go, and was a pillar of support for a lot of people. I clung to the celiac diagnosis as my "out"—a reason I did not fit into my current situation.

At that time, I was falling back into unhealthy habits while working on separating myself from unhealthy relationships and working through substance abuse. As a recovering addict, whenever things got hard it was always easier to surround myself with the things that would numb the thoughts, feelings, and realities of life. For me, my escape was drugs, alcohol and, surprisingly, too much work.

I often found myself surrounded by new friends—people who were more into the things one looks for to numb out reality so they can just get through life, show up to work, and maybe enjoy a laugh or two along the way. I knew I had once again surrounded myself with an unproductive, negative environment after another unhealthy relationship ended. I needed to find a way to break ties without breaking bridges.

Celiac made me different. First, it meant I could no longer eat what everyone else was eating. I had an excuse to no longer attend events, dinners, or gatherings that involved food. So much of what we do involves food, and many celebrations start with it. I had to make a healthy choice because I had to heal my body. I finally had a reason to remove myself from the scene and be more introverted without letting anyone down. I could no longer put things into my body that could potentially contain gluten (as if gluten were the unsafe part of using drugs). I now had a valid reason to say no to events where people who would negatively influence me could be in attendance. I became withdrawn and started sharing my new gluten-free life online: I reported on what I was eating and researching, and I shared my journey. I quickly realized that most of my friends and family had little interest in seeing what I was cooking and eating every day or what healthy lifestyle changes I was making or implementing, so I started sharing my journey on a separate social media account to find my people, my crew—people who were actively working to better themselves. I surrounded myself with a community who got it and motivated me to show up daily to be inspired to keep going.

The catch about social media is that it is part truths and only glamourizes certain portions of life. No matter how transparent you attempt to be, the grass just always seems greener on the other side. Often, we can be consumed by social media and the comparison trap. No one knew the hell I have dragged myself through and back to get to where I am now.

I have lived so many lives within my life, and I am continually growing as a person. I am a very self-aware, empathetic, compassionate, and driven woman, but for many years it was fear, doubt, guilt, and shame that ruled my life. There are so many people I know who are struggling mentally, financially, physically, or with addiction. But one thing I have learned is that we create our reality. It all starts with our mindset: you have to be good with "you" before you can be good with the world. All the experiences I have had have moulded me into the person I am with the beliefs I hold.

When I was about ten years old, my parents divorced. I took it hard. It was during this stage of life, however, that I started developing my confidence. I was close with my dad, but after the divorce, I felt as if I WERE THE MAN OF THE HOUSE. I helped my mom as much as I could with cooking and cleaning, and once I was old enough, I took a babysitting course so I could now watch my sisters after school. In school I was a "troubled" child." I attended most of the schools in our town by the time I went to high school. This constant transition had an impact on me in the long run. I was not the one who had a tight-knit group of lifelong friends; I was a social butterfly. Going to so many different schools in such a short time always made me feel out of place or not as connected to any group of friends. Our city was the fastest growing city in Canada, so as new neighbourhoods were built, school boundaries changed, and I would end up at a new school. The experience of going through five schools in about five years meant I knew lots of people and interacted with many different social circles but did not have a set social circle of my own. This experience has served me well as an adult, however. I have confidence interacting with strangers, asking questions and getting to know them and their stories. In the end it has made me adaptable to any situation life throws at me.

After the five schools in five years, I settled in one school for grades 4 through 8. However, when we were in grade 7, another new school was built, and most of my closest friends switched to the new school for my last year of elementary school. This last year was really rough. I remember not getting along with the other kids, not wanting to go to my grade 8 graduation, and I dreaded the idea of high school. I started smoking cigarettes in grade 8. I had a friend with an older sister who smoked, so we stole smokes from her. We felt pretty cool smoking her cigarettes. I also started drinking heavily in grade 8. My friends and I all had sleepovers on the weekends. We would stay up late, watch movies, and drink. I remember hanging out with my friends at our local mall and convincing strangers to buy us cigarettes and booze, or we would take what we could from our parents. I always had to get someone to buy for me because when I was growing up, I never saw my mom drink—ever. We did not have a drop of booze in the house. Everyone who knew us knew we had the "nicest mom" who never drank and never went out. She was always working or taking my youngest sister to her sports games and tournaments. My mom always gave us the best birthday parties and baked us fresh treats. She was the "good mom," so I was never exposed to drinking and partying at home. Nevertheless, I still had this anger in me, and I still wanted to just escape.

My weekend binge drinking came with violent outbursts toward my friends, which disconnected me even more. I was always at school or working, so I had money to buy myself alcohol and cigarettes. As I entered high school, I started smoking pot on a fairly regular basis, but my alcohol consumption was the most destructive. In grade 10, I did not get along with most of my teachers, which was also a challenge for me as I had been supported by my teachers so much in the past. Now, I struggled lots and no longer enjoyed school. I was not connected to any of the teachers, and I was less engaged with the learning. I was drinking more and more. Then, something happened that sent me into a pretty dark spiral, and the substance abuse only got worse. It was then that I started a ten-year spiral into what I call the dark years.

One summer night a friend invited a few people for a sleepover on her family boat that was parked at the town dock. We were excited! After school we got ready to head to the boat. The plan was that the four of us were going to have a couple of drinks and pass out after staying up late gossiping and having a girls' night together. We were eager to get together, but one of the girls had to work, so when her shift was done, my mom picked up the three of us with our bags and dropped us off at the boat. We were having a great time all hanging out until a random guy walked up to the boat and asked if he could come aboard. We got sassy with him and basically told him, "Yah, right, buddy. Get a life." We carried on with our evening, having the best of times, the four of us laughing and joking. The sun had set, and it was dark outside, and we saw the guy we told to take a hike approaching the boat. This time he was not alone . . . he was with a bunch of guys. They immediately forced themselves onto the boat. I instantly felt sick and terrified. We were outnumbered, and the energy on the boat was not comfortable. It was tense and full of unwelcome gestures and inappropriate passes.

By this time one of the girls was sleeping below deck. I knew I had to wake her and tell her that we were in a bad situation, so I went down to the cabin to tell her we needed to get out of there. As I began to explain what was happening, one of the men entered the room and slid himself between the two of us while making rude suggestions. My friend and I were just making eye contact with one another. My skin was crawling, and I was thinking, "What the fuck is happening, and how the hell are we going to get out of this?" More guys entered the room, and my friend said she had to go pee and started exiting the room. I sat down as she was leaving. One man put his arm around me, and I was frozen. Once my friend was out of the room, I popped up and said, "Let me go with her quickly, and I'll be right back. I can't let my friend go alone. Don't worry, we will be quick." As I exited the boat, she was gone. I could not see her anywhere. It was late now, and everything was closed. I remember screaming on the top of my lungs, "Help! Help! Help!" while running down the main street of our downtown, looking for my friend and for somewhere to call for help.

There was a sandwich shop that was normally open twenty-four hours a day, but it just so happened to be closed at that moment. Even though it was closed, I knew they were in there cleaning. I banged on the door, begging for help and to let me use the phone, telling them to call the police. Nothing. So, I kept running down the street. These moments replay over and over in my head in slow motion like a weird scene in a movie: the feeling of panic and being alone and wondering where I was while running down the street. What's going on? Is this really happening? What is happening to my friends right now? I remembered we had left two friends on the boat. I just kept running until I made it the two kilometres from the boat to the end of the road where there was another twenty-four-hour coffee shop. I could see my friend was there, and she told me she had called her parents to come pick her up.

The two of us headed back to the boat to tell the other girls that parents were coming. I can't be sure how long we were gone, but as we approached the boat, one of my friends was standing there screaming about what had occurred after we left. She screamed, "How could you leave me?" The guy who had had his arm around me when I left was there and yelled, "Your girl broke my nose!" The details are blurry, but the guys took off after that. I just remember lots of yelling, screaming, and crying until my friend's parents arrived.

We were brought in to give statements to the police. The men were arrested later that evening after an armed carjacking. I remember the police saying to us that the guys were bad and that they were known to the police. The police told us what neighbourhood the men were from and that we better not go near there because they would be out to get us. I don't remember much more. Eventually, we had to go to court and testify. I have blocked the whole experience. I can't remember any of that.

This was one of those moments in life that changes you forever . . . that safe little community, that perfect life where nothing terrible happens was not so real anymore. Bad stuff happens. There are bad people . . . and pardon me, but the cop taking my statement and telling me they might come back for us?!?

Afterward, I remember the four of us getting together for a sleepover and talking about what had happened. We all even collectively made a call to a kids' help phone to talk to someone. I don't remember any more other than we all drifted apart after that, or maybe I just drifted away.

Life went on. I started hanging out with some other girls I knew at school as well as some people from work. The partying and drinking increased, and now I was discovering other drugs. As my binge drinking continued, I had my next traumatic experience within a year. There was an all-ages event at a local club. My friends and I got together before the event and did some pre-drinking because we were underage. We went to the club and were dancing and laughing when suddenly I couldn't see any of my friends; I couldn't see anyone. I was circled by a group of guys who towered over me. They were bumping me around, so I tried to squeeze between a couple of them, but they kept me circled. I felt a hand around my hand, and all I could think was that they were the guys from the boat . . . they had come back, just like the cop had warned me. I left my body at that moment. I just stood there, praying that I wouldn't die. I knew what was happening. I didn't fight, I didn't scream, I just hoped I didn't die. It felt like time stopped, like I was stuck there, and it was never going to end. Suddenly I slammed back into my body. The feeling first came back to my leg. It was the dirtiest feeling no words will ever be able to explain. It started as a warm feeling and turned into an excruciating realization of what had just happened. Then, it was over, and the tight circle was gone—poof!—fucking gone back into the shadows. I became aware of myself again, of my body, and of where I was and my surroundings.

I ran full speed toward the exit, screaming on the top of my lungs like you see in a horror movie. I was about to run outside the building when a friend from school grabbed me, squeezed me, and told me to calm down, then demanded I tell her what had happened. The next thing I knew, I was being escorted by the police. Turns out I was assaulted in the only area of the nightclub where there was no video surveillance. The next thing I knew, I was being driven to the next town to be "processed" at the "sexual assault clinic." The only words that I can use to try and describe my mindset and emotional state are FEAR, ANGER, GUILT, and SHAME.

FEAR that it was the same guys from the boat. That they would come again, and that I would never really know who they were, where they were, or when they were coming for me. Fear that I was now in danger of an infectious disease. Fear about my safety and my family and friends' safety. Fear about what people would think; fear about explaining myself; fear about who to trust; fear of everything.

ANGER that this assault happened, that my friends were not around, that my boss terminated me as I called from a rape clinic, that I didn't fight back, that I let this happen. I was angry at the world.

GUILT that this happened to me because I had left my friends on the boat that night, and I finally got what was coming to me.

SHAME that I humiliated myself and my family and that I somehow deserved it. I shamed my family. I let something terrible happen to me.

Not long after this experience, something happened at school. The girl who had stopped me in the doorway and called the police that night at the nightclub said something to me that hurt me like nothing else. Maybe we were fighting and she said it in jest, but from that moment I believed that what she said was how everyone thought of me—that I had asked for it. That I deserved it. The moment those words came out of her mouth, I no longer cared about anything or anyone, especially at that school. I thought they all knew what had happened and were all talking about me. I separated myself from everyone and started doing more and more drugs.

I started hanging out with a couple of girls I knew growing up. However, as I drifted away from one group of friends to another, it almost justified the choice I was about to make because I knew these girls, and it got me away from all the judging eyes of the peers at my school. I knew they were into drugs, and if they were doing them, I could do them because we grew up together and were from the same place. In retrospect, I can see it was not such an unconscious choice to surround myself with these friends. It made drug use okay, justifiable, more realistic, and reasonable.

After a weekend with these girls, I was hooked. Ecstasy immediately became my substance of choice. I will never forget the night

I swallowed my first pill. I remember how scared I was. I did not swallow my pill until an hour after my friends did because I wasn't sure about it. I did not want to die, but I wanted to forget everything and have the best time. They had already been experimenting with Ecstasy, and I had never tried it before. I watched them take it and become happier, funnier people who suddenly enjoyed the simplest things in life: the colour of a wall, the sparkle in your eye, etc. Once I saw that they didn't die, I gulped it back with some blue Kool-Aid. I will never forget that shortly after I swallowed it, my friend ran to the sink and vomited her guts out. She assured me it was simply because of the food she had eaten and that we would all be okay. I was clearly alarmed. It was my first time trying Ecstasy, and I thought my friend had gotten a dirty pill. But she was certain it was just the food she had eaten and assured me I would be fine because she had had these pills before. Everything would be fine soon, and we were fine. Everything was suddenly much more than okay. Nothing mattered, everything was love and happiness, and from that moment I was hooked.

I quickly escalated from getting high every weekend to every day. I found friends from whom it was easier to buy my drugs, and it eventually got to the point that I was using regularly throughout the day in small doses so that I could maintain the high but be functional at school and work. The drugs were in our school, and my friends started to comment that I was using too much. Although lots of my peers were regularly getting high, it became evident that I was using more than my peers.

Soon, my income was not enough to support my addiction, and I was reaching out to friends to help me with a couple of bucks here and there. When I wasn't at school or work, I was out with friends. I was removed from school in grade 11 and told that I could not return until I had some counselling to deal with my problems. I started seeing a counsellor through my doctor and was in and out of school for a bit after that, but I ultimately left school altogether. The drugs did not stop, and the party went on. Eventually, the *shame* I felt every time I came home was way too much—the shame of looking into my mother's eyes, knowing I was lying to her, and knowing I was doing all the things she raised us not to do or be. She tried everything to keep me at home, but it was too late—I was gone. I knew everything, and I had been working for years and going to school, so I felt I could take care of myself. I left home and spent a while couch surfing with my boyfriend. I remember looking around at times and wondering how I got there and who all the people were. I was in places and with people you only see in movies. I would spend nights awake in a party house, high on drugs and cleaning, while strangers were passed out all throughout the place. I eventually got my own apartment so I could avoid shame by not having to face my mother every day and lie to her about still using.

I spent the next few years high, living in a make-believe happy land with a bunch of misfits. I was in and out of unhealthy relationships, each one of which I learned something valuable about myself. With each relationship came a breakup, a cleansing, and a purge cycle. I got rid of more belongings and focused more and more on myself, but I had to work not to fall back into unhealthy habits. I had been off drugs for several years and was moving up the ranks at work. I was slowly building something positive and creating little changes in my life outside of work to move toward a healthier life.

I lived with my sister for a while, and it was nice to get close again. I was able to make up for some lost time, to set better examples, and to support her in any way I could after so many years of not being around while I dealt with my demons. Moving away from the known and familiar to a safe space with my sister where I could focus on me was a game changer. It gave me the chance to take time to find myself again and connect with my reality.

After years of struggling and striving to pull myself together, I managed to pay off all my debts, rebuild relationships, and create a healthy, happy, sober life. I have an amazing guy in my life. He is the most thoughtful, stubborn, hard-working person in whom I see a lot of myself. He always wants to ensure the people around him are happy and well. He works hard and expects those around him to work hard too. He is an entrepreneur and is driven beyond belief. He constantly pushes me to light myself up to find what actually motivates and inspires me. He has empowered me to fully become myself. I am independent yet supported. I know I can ask for advice, and that I have an equal who will give me meaningful and constructive feedback. I know I have a partner who is not tying me down, holding me back, or stifling me, but one who is striving to grow alongside me, with me. Together!

After spending many years stuck in fear, anger, shame, and guilt, I was forced to focus on my health. The outbreak of psoriasis has debilitated the use of my hands, pushing me out of my addiction to work or using work as a place to hide from reality. It led me to be more focused on my health and recognize the stress I was putting on myself and my body. Then the celiac diagnosis further pushed me to evaluate my overall nutrition and health. When I finally started to deal with my emotions and stop numbing my feelings and was ready to change, my body started giving me trouble. I could have used that as a reason to fall back into depression, addiction, and the shame/guilt/fear cycle, but that trouble is what freed me, empowered me to learn even more about myself, and propelled me into a healthier life.

Now, instead of working hard, long hours and draining myself and those I love, my job as a virtual wellness coach is to first and foremost take care of myself, to make myself a priority and show up for "me" every day, and to give myself time to exercise, read, write, reflect, and release. By caring for myself first, I am able to INSPIRE others to work for their goals. No matter how bad it seems, they reach for their goals and get unstuck. I am able to EMPOWER people with the tools and resources to light.

I continue working through my personal healing journey with daily physical and mental health, while working with others to help people incorporate healthy lifestyle choices into their everyday life, including fitness, nutrition, mental health, personal development, and general wellness. I now choose to live as intentionally as I can. I pride myself on living mindfully. I reflect on each action and decision I make to see how it falls under one of these guiding principles.

MOTIVATE. INSPIRE. EMPOWER.

I hope to help people who may be in a dark season of their life by connecting them with support, resources, and community, while helping them build healthy habits and routines that support a healthy lifestyle. I strive to exemplify that you can thrive through the hard times to flourish into WHO YOU WANT TO BE. The hardest part of it all can be believing in yourself through the dark or challenging seasons of life.

Jessica Danford

Jessica Danford is an online personality and wellness coach known as GfreeWifey. She is a passionate advocate for the celiac and gluten-free community, serving on the board of directors for the Canadian Celiac Association. Dedicated to minimizing food insecurity on a gluten-free diet, she created #GFreeWifeyFoodBank in 2018. Partnering with local businesses and community leaders, Jessica advocates for and provides access to safe food. She is an effective community builder who brings people together to produce community cookbooks that empower people to share and live their best gluten-free life. Jessica's life experiences shaped her into a resilient and inspirational role model. Follow along on her website as she shares her gluten-free life as a diagnosed celiac living and thriving with rheumatic psoriasis.

f Gfreewifey

@gfreewifey

@jessicadanford

gfreewifey

gfreewifey.com

Thanks to my support network for believing in me. To my mom, Belinda, for always talking me off a ledge. To my dad for your hilarious sense of humour and no-BS advice. Even if I did not take it when you gave it, I listened. To my sister Alexis, I am glad we got closer with age and that we are able to help each other now. To Mark for constantly sharing your unique perspective with me and your belief in me. Your drive is inspiring and empowering. To Andy for spending your days and stories with me. I had a lot of great teachers at MDY, but I must say a special thanks to Mrs. Cindy Graham. I hope that sharing some of my story helps someone but also empowers my sister, Jamie, who is currently struggling with her addiction, to know she can recover too. You were my bestie. I'm sorry I was not the role model you needed. You have to keep shining in the dark. You can do it. Love ya all tons.

JANA ♡ WE HAVE NOT HAD A CHANCE TO MEET YET BUT DAVE WAS/IS A GOOD FRIEND OF MINE HE WAS LIKE THE BROTHER I NEVER HAD A GENUINELY GREAT GUY. I RECENTLY FOUND YOU ONLINE AND LOVE FOLLOWING ALONG YOUR CRAZY AMAZING MOMPRENURE LIFE. KNOWING DAVE AND FOLLOWING YOU ONLINE I KNOW YOU ARE A GREAT CANADIAN WOMAN TOO!! STAY HEALTHY HAPPY AND AMAZING BIG LOVE AND HOPE TO MEET YOU ONE DAY. I HOPE THESE STORIES" OF STRENGTH COURAGE PERSERVANCE EMPOWER YOU TO STAND TALL ON YOUR STORY AND KEEP BEING GREAT ♡

LOTS OF LOVE

JESSICA DANFORD

She Is

———— Humble

CHAPTER 10

BIRTH AND REBIRTH

Cindy Goch

When I was growing up, it seemed that every adult I met asked me, "What do you want to be when you grow up?" I always understood that they were not asking what I wanted to BE but rather what I wanted to DO (as a job). I never had an answer, and it was always implied that I should.

All I knew was that I wanted to have children. I wanted to be a mom. In fact, I used to tell people I was going to have ten children! My little sister and I played "Barbies" every Saturday morning, and I always had the same Barbie family: a mom, a dad, and their ten children. As clear as I was about having children, I was equally clear that dreaming of being "only" a mom was not enough, at least not in my family and in our social circle.

This was the '80s! Women had worked hard for equal rights.

We could be whatever we wanted to be. Roberta Bondar was a household name. We were encouraged to reach for the stars, quite literally, by becoming astronauts. In my family appropriate answers to the question "What do you want to be when you grow up?" consisted of "doctor," "teacher," "social worker," "police officer." The women's movement of the '60s and '70s had (rightfully) given women the power and opportunity to pursue any career they wanted. At the same time, it took away our opportunity to choose a simpler life. As a society, we have created an economic situation where a two-income home is necessary to maintain an adequate standard of living. We, as women, have lost our power to stay home and focus on our families should we choose to do so. It's also become socially unacceptable and almost looked down upon to make this choice. How many times have you heard a woman say, "I'm JUST a mom"? As a stay-at-home parent, I've experienced a sense of discomfort, almost shame, when checking the "stay-at-home," "homemaker," or "not-in-the-workforce" box, similar to what someone checking the "unemployed" box may feel. Though I feel this outlook is changing, the subtle meaning of this box has become "not contributing to society."

As I grew into a young adult, I ticked off the boxes: graduated university; established a successful career path; got married. I was still young, and I knew that I wanted to start a family, but I was concentrating on my career. Children felt like something far off in the future. And it felt that way until the day I went to the doctor's office for a random concern and she offhandedly made the remark that it was likely going to be difficult for me to have children. Like a blow to the gut, her words took the breath right out of me. I was not anticipating this news. It was one of those moments when the whole world became fuzzy. I could not pay attention to what she was saying. Her words seemed mumbled, like Charlie Brown's teacher: "ba ba ba ma blah." In my memory, I had tunnel vision—I only saw the doctor's mouth moving and everything else faded out. I was in a state of shock.

Walking to work after the doctor's appointment that day, I was completely preoccupied with grief. Two things were happening simultaneously: my mind was completely blank, void of all activity, but at the exact same time, thousands of thoughts were cycling even faster than I could grasp. I was flipping through the Rolodex in my mind, frantically looking for a solution. Two lessons have stood out for me from this exact time period. The first is that you don't know what you want until it is gone. The second is if someone tells me I can't do something, all of a sudden I want to do it one hundred times more (even if that means forgetting all my other goals), just to prove that I can—to prove I'm in control; I'm in charge. What I learned over the decades to follow is that, in fact, we are not in charge. Learning to surrender and letting go of control is ultimately what has led to happiness in my life.

During the months after my doctor's visit, people could see that something was wrong. Instead of presenting as my usual cheerful self, I was sullen, preoccupied, and devoid of light. I acted like a robot. And that was how I felt. I was completely empty and hollow, like my heart had left the building. A number of people came to me at different points, asking if I was okay. I just smiled and nodded. I had zero desire to discuss what was happening with anyone. One man I worked with quietly asked me if I was accidentally pregnant, thinking that might be the reason I was so upset. I couldn't believe it.

Even between my husband and me, there was very little discussion about what we were experiencing. I knew what a disappointment I was to him. I also felt like I was disappointing my parents who clearly wanted grandchildren. I felt embarrassed, isolated, scared, and worthless. I felt like a failure and like I was causing so much pain and loss to those important to me.

The doctor told me it was a good idea to try and get pregnant sooner rather than later. The baby-making race was on. This period was the first of the difficult times in my marriage. My husband and I had different work schedules—him on days, me on evenings. Finding a time that worked for both of us to be intimate was not easy. Weekends had always been a better time for us, but when you are on a mission to make a baby, your preferred schedule does not matter; it is your biological schedule that makes the rules. We both began to view intimacy as a chore, something that needed to be done on a specific schedule not of our choosing, much like the laundry or the grocery shopping.

The things helpful in baby-making, like fun, playfulness, spontaneity, and passion all went out the window and were replaced by clocks, thermometers, saliva analyses, and calendars. During this time, my husband grew more and more resentful of the systematic approach to love making. At the same time, I grew more and more resentful of his unwillingness to surrender to the schedule. Of course, the more resentment each of us felt, the less intimate we wanted to be. The less intimate we were, the more hopeless I felt. And then when we were intimate during the proper time of the month just to have my period come two weeks later, it was as if I had fallen off a cliff.

More than once I was completely convinced that I was pregnant. My breasts would ache, my appetite would change, and I just felt different. Then my period was late. I thought of purchasing a pregnancy test but held off. Under the surface, I did not want to face the possibility that I was wrong. It was fun to feel hopeful and joyful for a while. I remember sitting in the back of a concrete high-rise on a bench during my break at work. I was so sure that we had succeeded that time. I felt a sense of calm and tempered joy. It was not an ecstatic feeling in any way like I had experienced before but rather steady contentment, satisfaction, and a sense of everything now being okay.

When I got my period a week or so after, I was shocked. I could not believe how wrong I had been about my body. It occurred to me that I had possibly been pregnant, but it had not stuck.

I wondered if the Blackberry I had to carry on my belt for work could have done something to the embryo.

I wondered if the coffee I drank had done something to the baby.

I wondered if the frozen dinners I had eaten as a student had harmed my body.

I remembered the time I told my friends, "I am so unhealthy that I don't have to worry about birth control because how could I conceive?" I wondered if I had said those words and they were coming true now.

I remembered the time my teenage friend thought she might be pregnant, and I prayed the rosary all night, asking God to help her. I wondered if the thought had come into my head that I would sacrifice my fertility in order for her not to be pregnant. Had "HE" heard me? Did I cause this?

I worried the baby had actually been some cosmic mistake, put in my womb by accident, and when the powers-that-be figured it out, the baby was aborted because clearly, I was not cut out to be a mother; clearly, I was completely undeserving; clearly, I would be a train wreck of a parent.

It was a lonely, dark time. I could not tell anyone the thoughts that I was thinking; I knew they would just tell me how stupid I sounded. I knew that I would have to smile and agree with them in order to protect **their** feelings. I also knew that I was right. If I was deserving, the baby would have stayed—that was how things worked. I strongly believed that you get what you deserve, and you get what you work hard for. I was clearly working hard for a baby and therefore, since it was not happening, it could only mean I did not deserve it.

After a year of trying for a baby in Toronto, we decided to move to northern Ontario. It seemed like we were setting ourselves up for starting a family the "right" way. I thought that this explained everything not working over the past year—it was just not the right time. NOW we would be set up properly. Now everything would work out and a baby would appear shortly. Life clipped along. Then very unexpectedly, my father-in-law became ill and passed away before we could "give" him a grandchild. In a short time, we went from feeling like children to feeling like adults. We decided to continue trying to get pregnant and, at the same time, begin the process of applying to be adoptive parents.

The adoption process was intense and time-consuming. We filled out all the paperwork, shared our life stories, and put the most intimate aspects of ourselves and our marriage on the paper to be dissected by strangers. We attended training sessions and read books on adoption. At the same time, we were still actively trying to get pregnant. We waited. We waited for a call from the adoption agency, and we waited for my period every month. We waited and waited and waited for a call, or a sign, that we would be parents. The cycle of anticipation followed by disappointment continued. Even though I swore not to, each month I would trick myself into getting excited that this would be a month a baby would come. And each month, no baby.

At one point I decided that gaining weight might help me conceive, and this decision gave me an excuse to bury my emotions with junk food. Being a small and active person by nature, I went from 110 pounds to almost 150 pounds in a year. I told myself I didn't care. People assumed I was pregnant because of the weight gain. I told myself I did not care about that either.

Another year passed, then two. One day, completely by surprise, there was a voicemail on our answering machine that said, "You have a son." We drove to the adoption agency the next day, and within the hour, we met him: our son. He was the cutest little toddler we'd ever seen. We were instantly in love. Less than five days later, he was home. After trying to become a mother for years, I had become one literally overnight. I still experience butterflies in my stomach even thinking about that time now. There are no words to accurately describe the feeling. Every emotion ever named came into and out of my body on a rotating basis over those first few weeks.

I was one hundred percent invested in transitioning my new son and being the best parent possible by giving him every opportunity. We attended a weekly playgroup together. Each week I played on the floor with him and the children while the other moms sat at the tables socializing, and every week the topic of conversation would turn to birth stories. All the other women in the room had recently gone through the trauma and miracle of giving birth. Each mother took turns telling her pregnancy and birth story, and every week I felt completely alone and isolated. Not only was I an outsider in this community but I was an outsider in their experience. I had absolutely nothing to contribute to the conversation, so I said nothing. One out of ten times someone would clue into my pain. They would tell me, "You are so lucky you adopted your son and didn't have to go through pregnancy and birthing." I would fight back tears while trying to put on a smile for my son. I tried to hide my pain from my baby, but he knew. Each week after playgroup we would go home and his behaviour would be terrible. I felt like a sham and a horrible mother. But I went back each week for more, because like any mother, I placed my son's needs above my own.

After a year or so of playgroup, I became numb to my feelings surrounding the birth stories and could effectively block them out—or at least pretend to. I built up some rock-solid walls around my heart! I no longer felt close to tears on a weekly basis. I just concentrated on my son and had a good time. Then, the pregnancies started. It seemed like every mother attending the playgroup, along with my old friends from high school and university, along with seemingly every other woman I came across, was pregnant. Each week a new person would announce their pregnancy. Each week I would feel like I couldn't breathe, and an overwhelming sense of jealousy would arise. Sometimes (before I could stop myself), I wished that they had a miscarriage, just so they could know how much pain I was in. Then, because I had already considered my unchecked thoughts long ago had somehow caused my infertility, that old motto "be careful what you wish for" would come into my mind, and I would immediately be scared that somehow my wish might actually cause a miscarriage. My jealousy was very quickly followed by an enormous sense of guilt. It was just more proof of what a terrible human being I was to feel this envy and think these thoughts. More affirmation that yes, thank God, no child would be placed in my womb to inherit my terrible genes and be raised with such a monster of a mother who could be so resentful and jealous.

During that time, my son started drawing pictures of a mommy with a baby in her belly. Obsessively. All the time. Every day, multiple times a day. "Nice picture," I would say.

Parenting a child with attachment challenges or adoption trauma, much like dealing with infertility, provides the opportunity to face all your own shadows, your deep-seated feelings of inadequacy, and much more. At three, my son developed a habit of screaming, "me not love you" over and over again throughout the day. It was becoming very clear to me that I was not cut out to be a mother. My own son who I loved more than anything else I had ever met ever on earth did not even love me. I had also heard repeatedly the idea that "children choose their parents." It was so clear to me why I had experienced all these years of infertility: it was because I was a lousy parent—of course I never got pregnant. What soul in their right mind would ever *choose* me to be their mother?

Many times over the years I had been sure I was pregnant (or was actually in the early stages of a pregnancy). One of these times I was trying to enforce a timeout (which we had been advised to do) for my son who was now four. He was in the midst of a major meltdown and pulling on the door handle that I was trying to hold shut. He was screaming, throwing things, and shouting about how much he hated me. I, of course, felt awful and was crying, sobbing really. My physical body was taking a toll over trying to hold the door closed. All I wanted to do was comfort my son, but I had been instructed to be firm. To be consistent. To follow through. If I said he needed to go to his room, I had to make sure that he actually went there—never mind the hours of trauma we were both enduring to make it happen. I remember watching the whole scene unfold as if in a movie. My memory of that moment is from the viewpoint of looking down as the scene unfolded. I felt such disgust in myself. The next day, after a sixty-five-day monthly cycle, I got my period. I was not surprised in the least. I told myself that I had been pregnant for sure, but that baby saw my terrible parenting skills and got the hell out of there.

I sat on the toilet and cried for longer than I can remember. My eyes were red and swollen, and no amount of cold water splashed on my face could hide the evidence. I was completely empty, like I had cried every single tear I had inside to cry. I was hopeless. I gave up. I was completely resolved to the fact that I would never have another child, and the child I did have would grow up and leave me as soon as humanly possible. And I knew—I KNEW—that it was all my fault.

I grew as a parent over the next couple of years. I learned about attachment and trauma. I learned effective parenting methods for my own unique son. I learned that I had no local support system and had to cut myself some slack. I learned to not always listen blindly to professionals. I began to quiet the inner voice that was telling me I was unworthy and terrible. I began to feel confident about trying for baby number two.

Because we lived in northern Ontario, our only option for intensive fertility treatment was to travel down south. We decided to undergo treatment at a private fertility treatment centre in Toronto. It is a six-hour drive from our house to the clinic. One way. I started treatment in the spring, and I took the Greyhound. I went to the fertility clinic for the tests and to get the medication, then came home on the bus overnight, parented and was with my husband in hopes of conceiving. No luck.

After three months of this routine, the clinic recommended we try artificial insemination (AI). This treatment entailed me spending nearly my entire cycle in Toronto while they ran tests, gave injections, and waited for the right time to introduce the sperm. We decided to do two cycles of treatment over July and August when school was out.

During the course of the fertility treatment process, I got used to people touching, looking at, inserting instruments into, and studying my private parts. I had no sense of modesty or privacy left. When we went through the adoption process, strangers prodded into every intimate area of my life: my sexual preferences, my bank account, my previous sexual history, my relationship with my parents. Everything. Now here I was again, but this time it was the private areas of my physical body on display.

I began to view myself as a specimen. Having been a private and modest person before, I became accustomed to sharing the most intimate and personal details of myself. Even my body was free for display. On one occasion when I was going for an examination, I entirely forgot to put the little paper sheet they provide over my lower half. When the doctor walked in, there I was, completely naked from the waist down. The doctor was more embarrassed than I was and nicely handed me the sheet and instructed me to cover up. This event became a metaphor for how I felt during that year. Completely naked. Like my entire body, all my thoughts, and my entire life were on display. I was resentful of other couples who had the freedom and pleasure of living a private life and who could make decisions and carry them out without the entire world being a part of it. This feeling of being stripped naked both physically and emotionally has stayed with me until this day.

Since I lived so far away from the clinic, I had to stay in the city for long periods of time. There were times when I had to bring my son with me to the clinic. My husband was at home, six hours away, and I did not have any family or close friends in this entirely different city to help me.

Walking into the fertility clinic waiting room with a young child in tow is intense! I imagine it is what it feels like to be a millionaire walking into a village in a third world country while fiddling with your jewels. All eyes were on me, boring holes into the back of my head. The resentment and jealousy in the room were palpable. I understood. I had been there, struggling with my own jealousy, fighting back tears, feeling the guilt arising because of the emotions I was experiencing. But here I was. Instead of being accepted by my peers who were in the same situation, I felt like an outsider. Like I had more than my fair share. Like I should count my blessings, and that I had no right to be there seeking help.

It is possible that all this resentment and anger toward me was, in fact, a trick of my imagination. Being a sensitive person, I have had thoughts that everyone is talking about me or thinking terrible things about me. Knowing the resentment and uncontrollable jealousy—even anger and rage I had felt toward other moms when they announced they were pregnant—I knew first-hand how even the nicest, most caring and compassionate people could experience intense emotions directed at other moms. So I knew that everyone in that room was thinking terrible things about me like: "Who is she to want another baby?" "She should be grateful with the one she has!" "She is taking my place here." "It's not fair." Being a person who always cared a great deal about being liked, fitting in, and not taking more than my fair share, sitting there in that waiting room with a young child in hand was pure torture.

Being in Toronto by myself without my husband reinforced my belief that I was in this infertility journey all alone. I did not feel like I had anyone to confide in. I also did not feel like I had any practical support. During one course of our fertility treatments, it was necessary for me to give myself hormone injections. I was told to pinch the fatty part of my belly and then stick the needle in and press the lever. I remember being in my hotel bedroom and sitting on the edge of the bed. It was dark, and my son was sleeping in the next room. It was quiet. I sat there, leaning against the bed, holding the belly fat in my hand for at least twenty minutes while trying to work up the courage to jab the needle in. I've seen television shows about couples undergoing fertility treatments where the male partner happily and playfully jabs the female partner in the bum with the needle. It is often portrayed as a playful and intimate event. There are two people in the baby-making business together filled with joy, anticipation, and hope for the future. This scenario was the furthest thing from what I was experiencing. Eventually, I gathered up the courage to stick myself with the needle, and it was not so bad. Each needle after that one became progressively easier. I learned that I could do anything needed.

Month after month we went through the process of hormone therapy, fertilization, waiting, and disappointment. Then, in July, we did it! We got pregnant! I remember so clearly the moment I found out, like it is a scene from a favourite movie that I have watched twenty times. I was standing on a street corner in Toronto, outside of Java Joe's, drinking a cafe mocha. Well, I was trying to drink it, but it was too hot. The phone had rung while I was ordering the drink and the caller had left a message. I was holding the burning-hot cup of coffee in one hand while checking my voicemail on my little red Nokia phone. It had this little antenna on the top you had to pull up, and that was hard to do while holding a drink. I wasn't frustrated, though; I was in a good mood. The doctors had advised I could drink one cup of coffee a day, but to be safe I was drinking less than that. It had been a good few months since I'd had my favourite drink, a cafe mocha, and I was moments away from taking the first sip when I heard the message, "You conceived." I instantly forgot all about the coffee. A huge smile spread across my face. I let down my guard completely. Before I could stop it, the switch inside flipped from "cautiously optimistic" to "downright ecstatic." In that second it felt like every single molecule in my body started jumping around, like I could actually feel myself vibrating.

People often talk about near-death experiences being as if their whole life (their whole past) flashes before their eyes in just a second. I had this same experience in this moment, but it was my future that I could see. I could clearly see myself newly pregnant. I saw my belly growing. I saw myself telling my husband, and I saw how happy he was. I saw him doting on me and bringing me ice cream. I saw the way he looked at me, full of love, appreciation, gratitude, and admiration. I saw myself telling my parents and my sister. I saw how excited my mom was. I saw her shopping for baby clothes. I saw the look in my father's eyes, and how proud he was. I saw myself with a huge belly, sitting in a chair at my parents' house in the middle of a baby shower. I saw myself birthing my baby girl. It was always a girl for some reason. I saw myself bringing home my baby. I saw her as a toddler, a young child, a teenager, and an adult. I saw my grandchildren. I saw everything. I saw all of this, this whole entire vision, in the matter of a second because in the next second, I heard the rest of the message . . . "It didn't take," the secretary said. "It's what they call a chemical pregnancy."

Before I even knew about being pregnant, I had miscarried.

It was amazing. The entire city, all those skyscrapers and all the traffic started to spin in a circle around me. I thought I was going to faint. I didn't. I started to laugh. I laughed for quite a while, standing there, holding my coffee. People looked at me. Then I drank my coffee and continued with my day. I didn't tell anyone.

In September of that year, the doctors informed me that they did not recommend any more cycles of AI, and if we were going to proceed, the next step would be in vitro fertilization (IVF).

We decided to take a two-month break and weigh our options. The IVF procedure was quite invasive, and it would require more time in Toronto—this time during the school year when my husband was working and my son was in school. At that time there was no subsidy for IVF, so it came with a heavy price tag. We needed to decide how much money we could responsibly invest. We also needed to decide how many embryos we could responsibly implant. We decided on three. Triplets would be the most we could handle.

Someone once told me that "coincidence was just God's way of remaining anonymous." I believe it! At the end of September, through a long series of very random "coincidences," I happened to be chit-chatting with our adoption worker. She was telling me the difficult circumstances of most kids coming into care, and that it would likely take years for us to be matched again. "For example," she said, "just now a profile for a sibling group of three children under three years of age came across my desk. How are we ever going to find a home for a group of three kids under three?" I laughed and agreed with her. Yes, it would be a huge challenge to take three kids under three years of age.

I then went back to work on my computer. The words "sibling group of three kids under three" kept going through my head. One side of my mouth was trying to turn up into a half smile. I was finding it hard to concentrate on my work. I began daydreaming about what it would be like to have three toddlers. By lunchtime I was back on the phone with the adoption worker. "Send me their profile," I told her.

The rest is history. My husband was equally on board with applying for their adoption. I told the worker we were interested, and from that very moment it felt like my heart lived somewhere outside my body. It was with my children. After months of a selection process, we were chosen to be their family. We started the transition process, and by winter of the next year, they were home with us. The missing pieces of my heart came home. We went from being a family of three to a family of six! The next year their newest youngest brother also joined us, and our family was complete at seven!

Over the past twenty years, I have dealt with infertility. I've learned through the challenge of parenting children with adoption trauma. I've doubled the size of my family overnight and figured out how to effectively manage a household with five children under the age of six. I've addressed my own issues surrounding the status of "adoptive" parent. I've worked through the grief of not birthing my own children. I've worked through the conflicting feelings of anger, jealousy, and IMMENSE gratitude toward my children's birth mothers. What have I learned in all of this? I've learned that in many ways my desire to parent children grew out of a desire and need to parent and nurture my own inner child.

You would think adopting five children would cure my longing for pregnancy, but that is not true. Adoption, I've learned, is a "cure" for being childless, AND it is in no way a "cure" for infertility. After adopting all five children, I may have said I was happy with the size of our family and that I no longer felt a desire to get pregnant. The truth is that I was lying. It took years of work within myself to come to terms with being "barren."

During the course of my journey with infertility and adoption, I was consistently harder on myself than I would be on my worst enemy. The things I said to myself inside my head and my unwillingness to cut myself slack over the very heavy emotions I was feeling are worse than I would treat anyone else in the entire world. The game changer for me was learning to be my own best friend. Even more than that, I learned to nurture and parent myself first. I learned to treat myself the way I would treat the child I so desperately wanted. After all, we "adults," it turns out, are really only little children inside grown-up bodies. The more I allowed myself to be kind and nurture myself, the more I was able to be kind to and nurture my children, and the more I was able to let go of the desperate struggle to birth a child of my own. Every day now I'm in the process of rebirthing myself, and that, it turns out, is what I actually needed all along.

Cindy Goch

Cindy Goch is a northern Ontario girl to the core. She loves camping, swimming, being in nature, and all things outdoors. Cindy is the mother to five young children who light up her life. She is a certified yoga instructor and numerologist, and she has a passion for philosophy and spirituality. Throughout her adult life, Cindy has reinvented herself many times, from being an academic to data analyst to yoga instructor to parenting coach and more. Currently, Cindy is taking some downtime to rediscover her passions and wait for a sign leading her way to the next adventure.

Cindy loves working with women and families using an array of modalities to help them find the most peace and ease in their lives. She is currently working on a full-length novel themed on the challenges of parenting children with different abilities.

cindygoch

@cindygoch

Cindy Goch

www.cindygoch.com

cindygochwrites@gmail.com

I would like to dedicate this piece to my own mother, Darlene. Before I was born, I looked around for the most compassionate, hard-working, and loyal woman I could find and chose very well when I picked her. She is a fierce advocate for all children and has always had my back. She has supported me, while at the same time trusting me to make the right decisions. Thanks, Mom, for teaching me how to mother both my children and myself.

She Is

—— Bold

CHAPTER 11

BREAKING THE SILENCE

Liz Pracsovics

*"The process of waking the inner creator
and setting her free was a long labour of
finding and trusting my voice—painful, scary,
bewildering, frustrating, but magnificently
worth it."*

SLEEP AND THE SILENCE OF SELF-DENIAL

They say everything becomes clearer in hindsight. Looking back over the last few years and marvelling at my journey to consciousness and healing, it is as though my life before these years was spent in the shadows of sleep and silence. In fact, only a part of me was silent and asleep—my independent voice and creative spirit.

The Big Sleep was not quiet or restful. It was full of melodrama and recurring nightmares. I thrashed about in a dreamlike maelstrom of random life choices, as my frustrated creativity, yet to find an outlet, struggled to manipulate my environment to provide the fulfilment I could not find within myself.

During the early years in England, after suffering an agonizing, repeatedly broken heart in my late teens, I drifted for a decade after school, never allowing myself to settle into a long-term job or relationship. Resisting commitment and loss of independence, I was also deathly afraid of suffering or inflicting more heartache. Constant shift and restless energy were my norm. I was a rolling stone to which nothing much stuck other than some very special friends who single-handedly worked to keep our friendships alive. I changed jobs and partners as often as my socks, avoiding obligation, responsibility, and conflict, and impulsively embarked on ill-thought-out adventures at the first glimpse of opportunity. Moving my act to Bermuda, a remote and unlikely destination where absolutely no one knew me, quenched what I saw as my thirst for novelty and discovery. In fact, it filled my repeated need to flee.

When I met my future husband a year later, our whirlwind romance and precipitous wedding appeared to fit right into my carefree lifestyle. I deluded myself with visions of happily travelling the world with a footloose partner who seemed to embody the freedom from societal norms and expectations that I craved. Needless to say, my rose-coloured glasses were unceremoniously ripped from my face by, in quick succession, a tubal pregnancy, emergency surgery, and the shock of a bona fide for-real pregnancy within three months of our wedding. It felt as if my life were over. We had no plans to have a child, and I was in no way prepared for motherhood. I couldn't be sure I even wanted to bring a child into the relationship. Against the odds, I had a textbook-perfect pregnancy and a healthy eight-and-a-half-pound girl child. I glowed with health, in stark contrast to the battle my ego was waging with itself. It felt like the ultimate loss of freedom. I blamed my husband, and my libido shrank to zero. I was so disconnected from myself as a fertile woman that I struggled to unearth any spark of maternal instinct. All I felt was fear and the huge responsibility of keeping this miniature human being alive. I was isolated from my family on an island far from home. I knew no one with children. I didn't know about the village—the village that was supposed to be there to support me. No one had told me about the village. I didn't even know to look for one.

I soon discovered I barely knew the man I had married. Instead of us linking arms on the pathway to parenthood, I felt separated from him by my physical female experience and my hormonal, emotional turmoil. He was attentive enough of our daughter, but neither of us knew how to, or even that we should, take care of me. In our ignorance, we added another child to the mix. For this pregnancy, there was no time for self-nurture with a demanding toddler ruling my life. After my son was born, tiny and three weeks early, I was soon exhausted, depleted, emaciated, and clinging to sanity. After several years away from work, I had lost all the personal autonomy I had felt in my now-interrupted career. I struggled to embrace my new role as a mother and had lost sight of my own dreams, needs, and self-development.

Things did not improve when I returned to work after four years of intense child-raising. An all-time low arrived, a dark night of the soul, after an unplanned walkout from my full-time job with a volatile litigator. I had been with the firm a little over two years and had fought to get a work permit for the position. As an expat on the island, I had to prove to the government that I was better than any local with similar credentials. It was my first permanent job after putting our kids into daycare and wrestling through a year of temporary jobs at minimum wage to squeeze myself back into the workforce. Walking out was not really a stellar idea. What I did not understand at the time was I had just manifested a classic adrenal response to stress—running away. This, of course, was my pattern.

My abrupt life change forced a shift in my perspective and led to some much-needed counselling. It also resulted in my first prescription for antidepressants. At the time, this medication was an essential step for my survival. The desperation, depression, and destructive patterns that had become my drumbeat were quite literally causing paralysis. I could not make a decision. My focus was gone, and my mind was overcast with heavy clouds. Breathing was something I had to remind myself to do. My body rebelled with painful back spasms that left me unable even to lift my arms. I was completely severed from my emotional, creative, and spiritual body, feeling only the physical and psychological pain of the disconnection.

For a few months, rest, relaxation, the absence of stress, and medication helped me reclaim some vitality, and there were unexpected bursts of creativity. I joyfully threw myself into designing and sewing Halloween costumes, delighted and surprised myself with the results, and marvelled at how alive this creativity made me feel. Looking back, this experience was a divine kick in the pants to take note of what made me happy. Sadly, responsibilities, self-judgment and self-denial took over too soon. I returned to work, and once again, there was no room for any self-nourishment or creative expression that did not contribute to food on the table, clothes in the closet, and the immediate needs of my growing family. Unsurprisingly, I continued with antidepressants, just to keep the lid on my Pandora's box of frightening emotional baggage.

So completely submerged in marriage, motherhood, work, and striving to make ends meet, I had no idea who I was or what I needed to thrive. A niggling awareness that this life was not what I had signed up for—that I was somehow cheating my destiny—hovered in my peripheral vision, but I had become adept at ignoring it and pushing it aside. The need to keep the peace, stay safe, and cling onto the security of marriage and work as a means to preserve the status quo completely drowned out my inner voice.

I now recognize that inner voice as my Wild Feminine screaming to be heard, raging at her repression, white-hot with anger at
being silenced for so long. What I had not bargained for were the
results of her repression—chronic pain and persistent depression.
Unpacking the patterns, I remember a recurring nightmare of trying
to scream and being unable to make a sound. As a product of the
culture of belittling, of keeping women quiet and in the corner, my
inner voice barely knew she wanted to be heard. Keeping my mouth
shut became almost a badge of honour. Just how much unfiltered
human input can I smile and nod through without giving a hint
of my inside world—the conversation between my inner listener
and my inner critic? I was so proud of the steely self-control I was
able to exert upon myself, and the easy-going, amenable, non-judg-
mental persona I was able to project that I hardly ever expressed
my true opinion. It was self-denial at its finest and saintliest. It was
also the result of an overriding need to be universally accepted and
acceptable, and to avoid conflict at all costs. I tried to be "nice"
no matter what occurred to the point of completely squashing
my own needs in case I should come across as high maintenance,
demanding, difficult, or in other words, "unfeminine."

"She has such a lovely personality!"

"She must be a saint."

I heard myself described in these ways by friends and family
members. Let me just unpack what perhaps they were really saying
and seeing: She lets people get away with treating her like dirt. She

appears to be so amenable and forgiving of others that she allows her own opinions, desires, and wishes to go unspoken. Worse than that, she becomes almost unaware she has desires and wishes that are hers and not just what she thinks others expect her to have. She denies her need to be heard, valued, and respected by those close to her to the point where she accepts inconceivable wrongs without flinching or blinking. She will even take on these slings and arrows, believing they are somehow her fault.

There is no glory in being called a saint. None of us wants to wait in the wings to be rewarded in heaven or the next life for denying our needs in this life. For saint, read doormat.

Each time I ignored my own needs and silently absorbed a dismissal of my feelings, it led to a little bit more dying inside. By allowing others too much space to be who they were and to hurt me if they wanted, I entirely abandoned myself and buried any aspirations or dreams of my own.

FINDING MY VOICE

Fast-forwarding through another decade, we uprooted our little family from Bermuda and moved to Canada, bought a house, found jobs, entered a whirlwind of family reunions, kids' activities, PTA meetings, teenage angst, and finally waved our son off to university. All this time I continued to stifle my inner voice and creativity. The use of antidepressants to stay afloat just became who I was, and all I expected to be, although I kept it well hidden from family and friends. Even my husband would have failed a skill-testing question on my medications.

In trying to fit into another foreign environment, make new friends and be accepted, I became tremendously busy doing a whole slew of things I really didn't want to do—a result of poor boundaries, being "nice," and saying yes when I really meant no. My calendar was full, but my soul was empty. A Brit by birth and by nature, I was naturally reserved and private about my personal life. "Britishness" also precludes self-promotion, frowns on complaining, and encourages stoicism. By maintaining an unruffled and polite surface, apologizing a lot, and never sharing too much of myself, I excelled at being a decorous Englishwoman but failed miserably at being me. Such careful guarding of my inner world inevitably made me lonely, even when among friends. I was unable to share my authentic self that I had hidden for so long, away from scrutiny and much too vulnerable and afraid to be seen and heard.

My inner dialogue went something like this: Why would anyone listen to me? How do I know anyone is interested? Do I even have anything of value to say? Where IS my voice? When I open my mouth in public, people talk right over me. I'm softly spoken by nature. To make myself heard, I have to raise my voice to an uncomfortable degree. But is it uncomfortable because I'm pushing it or because I don't feel worthy of attention? Or is it my dread of criticism, judgment, or upsetting someone that keeps me quiet?

And so I remained silent, but I ached to be heard.

My journey to finding my voice began at a pain-relief clinic I walked into one desperate day. I had debilitating back and shoulder pain—the result, I believed, of various minor but unresolved injuries. From chiropractic to physiotherapy to massage, nothing had given any lasting relief. The massage therapist who took me under his wing planted the idea that not all my pain was the result of physical trauma. Working on an emotional level, in an environment of complete non-judgment, I was finally able to dissolve some of the stress that held me in its grip. I began to dismantle the trifecta of anxiety, depression, and fear that kept me in a holding pattern of self-sabotage.

The process of opening my heart and mind to another human being without being judged or lectured to was unaccustomed but cathartic. I stepped cautiously into a world where the boundaries between body, mind, emotion, and spirit ceased to be so rigid; a world that promised new possibilities for healing and living in alignment rather than in conflict with myself; a world that celebrated spirituality, a heart-centred morality, and relating to our fellow humans with compassion rather than criticism. This was a world where I wanted to live.

Opening my mind also opened my life, attracting more people and opportunities that encouraged my expansion into this new universe. I dropped deeply into myself with a holistic healer versed in Eastern medicine who taught me ways to release my physical pain by acknowledging and fully feeling the grief and anger that I was holding in my body. I immersed myself in yoga and meditation, and I found an empowering and supportive women's circle. I learned that self-love and self-care do not equal self-ish.

With a new sense of self-worth, and lots of practice, I started setting healthy boundaries for myself. I was finally able to say no to some of the obligations that had taken over my life, creating more space for finding activities that nurtured my soul. Most importantly and significantly, I began connecting with my long-neglected need to create. It became clear to me that keeping my creativity bound in the shackles of self-judgment was not only a shame but also self-destructive. Moving way beyond my comfort zone, I bravely signed up for a women's music weekend. I knew not one of the thirty women at the retreat and was wracked by self-doubt—I couldn't possibly measure up to these enormously talented musicians, singers, and songwriters. It proved to be, however, an ecstatic weekend of joy, singing, and self-discovery. Through a guided meditation into a creative stream, I wrote my first song. I am still learning to accept my singing voice enough to sing my song, and I struggle with the logistics of writing music, but there it is. I wrote a song!

Diving deeper into my creative well, I took some drawing lessons and found that I could, in fact, draw; it is a lurking talent long ignored and denied. My mother and my daughter were the artists, not me. Drawing took me right out of my left-brain anxiety and into a right-brain focus and flow. Letting go of what I believed something should look like, bypassing logic centres, and drawing what I actually saw was a hugely liberating experience. I was literally bypassing thought and mental processing. The reward of producing something beautiful in this way made my heart sing. I later found more bliss in abstract painting, freeing myself from line and form and perfection. This, for me, was pure wild creation, pure freedom. I love my creations, but I am not invested in another's opinion of them. True freedom from a constant need for approval generates the space to explore and push the boundaries of my creativity. This creative expression is what I was meant to do.

✳ ✳ ✳

I am now two and a half years into a medication-free life. I finally shattered the cycle of pain and depression. I am stronger, I am using my voice, and I no longer need to be a victim of circumstances that appear to be beyond my control. I am learning to sink into and trust my intuition. When I heard about this book, this incredible collaboration of women writers, I knew I was being guided to contribute my story. The serendipity of time, place, person, and project coming together as they did could not be ignored. Writing is the next piece of my puzzle. As far back as grade school, my strength lay in words. My gift was expressing myself in writing. However, my inner critic and fear of failure suppressed the natural growth, nurturing, and sharing of this gift. I never felt qualified, and I never believed I had what it took to be a writer. And now, here I am. Writing and sharing. My story is not finished. This is life after all, and I am a gloriously flawed human being. The effort of using my voice and approving of myself continues to be raw and real. Every day brings a new challenge, or more often, an old challenge that refuses to stay locked in the closet and likes to break out and dance around in its underwear. But my resolve is fierce. I will not go back to the silence of self-denial or the detachment of keeping a chemical lid on my emotions. I have given myself permission to be unapologetically me; permission to do what comes naturally, without self-consciousness or concern over judgment or ridicule; permission to be a musician, an artist, a writer; permission to express myself fully, freely, and passionately; permission to step into the fire of my creativity and let it burn. Like the legendary phoenix, I am rising from the ashes of my silent life of self-denial, ready to fly and sing and show my burning colours to the world.

Liz Pracsovics

Born and bred in the UK, the only child of gregarious, philanthropic parents, Liz Pracsovics mostly shared her early living quarters with foreign students from all corners of the globe, in emergency accommodation while they found their feet. School holidays were spent visiting family friends in Europe, sailing lakes, rivers, and coastlines of the UK in boats borrowed or rented, or getting dragged to youth camps, church groups, and discussion forums closer to home. Leaving this uber-compassionate, multicultural, sometimes exhausting environment, she grooved, studied, and air-popped away her twenties in the City of London, skipping out from time to time to crew small sailing vessels around Spain and Africa and the blue waters of the Atlantic. After emigrating to Bermuda as a single white female with a job, meeting and marrying, creating two fascinating human beings, and finally landing in Canada, she learned what it means to grow roots. Her varied career in publishing, travel, and law led her to realize her most authentic path lies in giving her creative side a voice. Finding a new spiritual framework for her soul and a community of like-minded soul mates, she transformed from a long-suffering legal assistant into a reiki master, yogini, natural health nut, women's circler, artist, musician, and writer. A self-described "chronically late bloomer," she proves we are never too old to discover our gifts and reinvent our lives.

f liz.pracsovics

◎ @whitewidow2211

▸ @SagenTyme

This treatise on mental, emotional, and spiritual health is dedicated to my late aunt, Doreen Ashton, of the Fair City of Perth, Scotland, UK.

She Is

——— Beautiful

CHAPTER 12

ESMERELDA AND THE GOLDEN NUGGETS: MY JOURNEY THROUGH WIDOWED PARENTING

Marny Williams-Balodis

I am ready! My Kleenex is packed. The waterproof mascara is on. I have cried pre-tears in preparation for today, and I have strategies in place for the aftermath. I have mustered all the energy I can in order to make it through the evening with grace and style. Tonight is not the night for me to lose my cool and have an emotional breakdown. Tonight is a celebration.

I'm sitting in the auditorium about to watch my son's high school graduation ceremony. This is a day I couldn't have imagined fifteen years ago.

I sit and remember the million moments that led up to this one. I remember the doctor telling me this isn't good. I remember the nurse bringing me toast to eat. I remember the looks in the eyes of those around me. I remember his last words: "I Love You." I remember feeling his last heartbeat on my hand. I remember turning my head one final time to look at him as I left the hospital.

All these memories made up the unimaginable reality that had become my life. I was a widow and solo parent the week before my thirty-first birthday. My son was three, my daughter three months. How was this my reality?

I don't remember how I told my three-year-old his dad had died. I don't remember the words. I don't remember when or what his reaction was. I do remember the heartache I felt. The pain in my chest. When I hugged him, I wanted to embrace him and wrap him in bubble wrap and protect him from all the ugliness of the world. I desperately wanted to turn back the time and go back to what my life was just six weeks prior.

But I couldn't do any of this. I couldn't take away my children's pain. I couldn't bring their dad back or their innocence. Their world had been radically altered in ways I couldn't fathom. I couldn't even begin to imagine what their future would look like or start to understand their pain. All I knew was the agonizing injustice and grief of having to find a life without Keith in it.

I'd never faced a grief like it before. I had no idea what to expect or how to manage it. What I quickly learned was grief is a force that I could never have imagined. It takes over fully and completely. It's all encompassing. It's exhausting. It wanted my attention and sucked all my energy. It is impulsive, demanding, and spontaneous. It is something that I couldn't predict, and no matter how much I tried to control it, grief had its own agenda.

Grief took so much more away from me than just my husband. The world as I knew it before cancer and his death no longer existed. With four words, my world was no longer. "You have terminal cancer." This new world that I was now living in felt foreign and unsafe. I couldn't relate to others, nor them to me. What I knew to be true wasn't anymore.

Grief changed who I was. Everything I had envisioned for our future together and with our children was also taken away. Hopes and dreams for our life together were taken when he died. My grief also meant I had to redefine myself and all those visions I had.

Grief changed who I was as a parent and took me out of the running for the award of "Parent of the Year!" I was no longer a fun, carefree parent who laid down on the carpet and played Hot Wheels. I never brought out the Barbies I had as a kid and shared them with my daughter. My patience level was near non-existent. It wouldn't take much for me to lose my shit, and most times when I did, it would be followed by a round of apologies or extra hugs and cuddles. I was pissed at my reality. I was pissed I had to parent alone and that there was no one with whom to share it.

My dreams for my future never included being a solo widowed parent with two young children needing care.

Solo parenting meant everything was my responsibility. From

diapers to discipline, from meals to laundry, anything that needed attention was up to me. You name it, it was my job to do it. All the moments, be they amazing, arduous, miserable, or triumphant, were also mine to carry. Alone. If I was having a rough day, I was the only one who could try and work my way out of it.

My parenting became what I call "very grey." My kids got away with a lot just because I didn't want to deal with any aftermath of discipline. I heard a wise parenting expert say to make sure your kids' punishment doesn't turn out to be yours. I certainly felt like I had been punished enough and didn't want to add anymore.

I was scared for our future. I worried about how I was going to get my kids to university. I worried about how Keith's death was forever going to change my kids, and I worried about what those changes would look like. Would they need hours and hours of therapy in order to cope? Would I? Often, my worries were so far into the future that I had to remind myself to stay present. I needed to remember to feed my kids lunch—if I didn't do that, I wouldn't have to worry about university!

Time showed me I needed to develop self-compassion. I was given the impossible job of navigating solo parenting combined with young widowhood, and I had no instruction manual. I didn't know how to live this life, and others didn't know how to support me. I was alone, fumbling in the dark and just trying to keep afloat.

One day I had a revelation. I spent most of my time fighting my grief. I didn't like it, and I didn't like how it made me feel, so

I worked hard at ignoring it, trying to push it away and getting mad at it. But no matter what I did, grief was still there, staring me back in the face, almost taunting me. I realized I needed to work with my grief and not against it. So, I gave my grief a personality. I really should have named it, but I wasn't as insightful back then. If I were to name it now, I would probably call it Esmerelda! Don't ask me why that name—it just fits.

I looked my grief, Esmerelda, in the face and said, "I guess you aren't going anywhere. No matter what I do, you are always there, staring back at me." I decided that I needed to embrace her. I picked up Esmerelda and put her on my shoulder to carry as we looked toward the future together. Without grief constantly in my view, my outlook on the world changed. I stopped fighting grief and started figuring out how to work with it and maybe even learn from it. It truly altered the lens I looked through. I felt lighter and somehow more motivated to keep on moving through this grief journey.

Don't misunderstand me—feeling lighter didn't actually change the devastation, and certainly not when it came to my kids. No matter how overwhelming my own grief was, it was still easier than watching my kids grieve. I had to acknowledge that I could never understand what it was like to have a parent die and then grow up with that story. It wasn't my story—I was the widowed parent, and they were the grieving children whose dad had died.

People say time heals. I'm not too sure who said it, but there is some truth in it. But time doesn't heal if we don't work at it. As I tried to work through my grief, I eventually learned that I had a strength that I didn't know existed. When Keith and I went hiking in the mountains, his body had an uncanny ability to go faster and breathe more deeply as the elevation increased. My body, on the other hand, seemed to get more exhausted and my breathing more laboured. We would ultimately go our separate ways and then meet up on the way back down. He always told me that you can push your body more than you think you can and that it will respond. Grief made me stretch myself beyond my comfort zone. Somewhere out of this experience, I gained a strength, a stubborn independence that gave me the courage to try for one more day.

Being a parent is one of the most humbling experiences we can have. There is nothing that can prepare us for the worry, joy, fear, and triumphs that come when our child is born. We are forever a parent.

Being a widowed parent to grieving children brings even bigger worries and fears combined with joy and triumphs. What few "how-to" books there are for parenting, there are even less for widowed parenting.

So many of my parenting moments felt like out-of-body experiences. I would catch myself making statements and then ask myself, "Did I really just say that? Did that combination of words just come out of my mouth? Who says this shit?" Apparently, I do!

Never did I imagine having to explain cancer to my kids or

teaching them what it means to be dead. In between reading *Goodnight Moon*, I would read *It's Okay to be Sad* and *When Dinosaurs Die.*

So many times I cried to sleep with my kids. I would tell them stories about their dad—the good, the bad, the ugly, and the hilarious. As I shared, I watched them closely to see how they were reacting. Watching their body language to know when they had had enough or were curious for more was one of the many new parenting skills I developed.

None of these realities were in the *What to Expect the First Year* book. No chapter told me how to cope with their tears—tears I thought would be about scraped knees, troubles at school, and broken relationships, not tears because their dad died.

Somehow, I instinctively knew the importance of modelling healthy grief to my kids. They needed to see that it is messy, emotional, and exhausting and that it requires asking and receiving help. It means we must welcome vulnerability as we learn how to live in a world that just doesn't make sense anymore.

Some days I was brilliant, and others, not so much! Patience was something I had to foster. The constant repetitive questions about Dad, where he was, when he was coming home, were so trying. One of my "prouder" moments was when I got mad at my kid because all he wanted to do was see his dad and I yelled, "We'll go find him," only to have him yell back, "I don't know where he is." Momma guilt was rampant and often left me curled up in tears on the bathroom floor and begging for this nightmare to end.

Believe it or not, during all these ugly parent moments, I began to trust in my strength—the strength that Keith tried to teach me on those hikes. Deep down I was learning that I could do it and that somehow, we were going to figure this grief stuff out. Not only did I realize this strength in me, but I also began to see the same strength in my kids.

As time passed, I was able to open my eyes and my heart without guilt to see what my amazing kids were teaching me. Their lessons were subtle. I could have easily missed them, and I have no doubt there were many I did miss. However, there were also some astonishing moments, or as I call them now, golden nuggets—unique expressions of grief for their dad that had the ability to both fill my heart and completely flatten me.

In grade 5 my son developed a Grief Wizard kit with hope of helping his peers who may also be grieving the death of a parent, and seeing his words "Death & Dying Equal Happy Living" left me speechless. I had so much pride, and my tears silently flowed as I watched him present this project.

In grade 8 my daughter and I went on a trip to Calgary that I called "Meeting Your Dead Dad." I knew she wanted to build a relationship with the man she called an imaginative figure rather than her dad. I had witnessed her pain and heard her anguish over not having gotten to know him. This trip, to walk in his footsteps, was my way to support her in continuing to build this relationship.

It was surreal. Who does this? Who plans a trip like this? Again, apparently I do!

Being present to her heartache as she learned about all she would never know first-hand . . . there truly are no words to explain how this felt as her mom. All I do know is that during every moment of this trip, I watched my daughter grow in confidence and maturity. She left Calgary feeling lighter and more assured in her grief. It was an awe-inspiring experience to witness.

These are just two examples of the golden nuggets I got to be present for—there are so many more I could share.

These golden nuggets, as impressive as they were, meant I had to find a way to straddle the vortex between opposing emotions . . . emotions that we don't typically find together. The pride I felt in my kids for what they were doing combined with the sad reality of why they were doing them continued to create caverns filled with conflicted emotions that I had to navigate.

Many of these moments occurred years after Keith died. Most I processed on my own. Our society has a misunderstanding of the everlasting impact of grief and how it does or does not change. I feared the judgment of others and of myself. While there is truth to the statement that grief changes over time, it doesn't directly correlate to it becoming easier. I had to learn to live with it and continue to let it teach me. The idea that I would have to explain to anyone why I had "ugly cries" months and years after Keith's death just added a pain I didn't want. So, I learned to navigate these caverns on my own.

Over the years I have learned and now understand that kids' grief changes as they grow and understand more. Their questions change, and their curiosity changes. They want to know more—they want to have their own relationship with their parent. Parenting through the weeds and unknowns of your children's grief is in some ways like waiting for the other shoe to drop. You never know when a grief-burst might show up for each of them or for yourself. I certainly didn't want to live waiting for it, but grief does sit in the background, sometimes quietly and sometimes showing its face in a full force that knocks you to your knees.

Hindsight makes us brilliant. When I reflect, I now know that I would have done things differently, but at the same time, I wouldn't have changed anything. I didn't understand grief. I didn't understand what children's grief looked like. I didn't know how it would evolve or that it would evolve differently in each of my kids. All I knew was that I needed to engulf them in love. I did everything I could to protect, love, provide for, and encourage my kids. I did my absolute best, and I continue to do just that. If that is what I am doing, then how can I do it differently?

Today is a day that I could never have imagined fifteen years ago. I find myself in one of those emotional vortices of grief. Saddened by my past. Proud of my present. Wondering about my future. But I also know as I sit here that I am surrounded by love and am blessed to have my new life. I use the Kleenex I packed to discreetly wipe away my silent tears in hopes no one will see.

But I can feel my daughter's eyes watching me! I have become an expert at breathing through my mouth and not snorting up those grief tears!

As proud as I am of myself, I am in awe of my kids. My son is walking across the stage to receive his diploma, about to launch into adulthood. He is brilliant, he is handsome, he is successful, he is caring, he is awesome.

My daughter sits beside me and beams with pride for her brother. She, too, is going to set the world on fire. She has a compassionate and empathetic heart that will have a huge impact on those she touches. She is a fighter.

My family now includes my husband Dave and our son, Nathan. They are my blessing. I am beyond grateful.

To have all these blessings because Keith died feels weird. From an inconceivable tragedy, we have built a new life—an amazing life. I am a completely different person because of Keith's life and death, and so are my kids.

Fifteen years ago, I could not have dreamed of this life. Today, I am living it.

I know there will continue to be moments when my grief will reappear. The fact that it sits quietly and comfortably perched on my shoulder doesn't scare me like it once did. I am okay that we walk together and look through that shared lens together. I am okay with all that grief has taught me.

So, when it appears and says, "Remember me?", I will reply with "Oh, Esmerelda—how could I ever forget!"

Marny Williams-Balodis

What the world had planned for Marny Williams-Balodis was not what she wanted. Who wants to join the widowed club at the age of thirty with a three-year-old and three-month-old?

Shortly after the death of her husband, Marny had a seed planted in her soul, and she knew that one day she wanted to give back to the widow community. When the time was right, she co-founded The Hummingbird Centre for Hope—a charitable organization that supports widowed parents and their young families.

Marny not only has her personal story, but she has continued to expand her knowledge in many areas. Her proudest educational accomplishments include being certified in Thanatology: Death, Dying, and Bereavement through ADEC and holding a certificate in Grief and Bereavement from Western University in Ontario. She also provides bereavement care for Henry Walser Funeral Home. She has had the honour of companioning grieving families since 2005.

Marny has developed a level of empathy and passion that is key to her success. Being present in other people's intense emotions is a legacy that came from the death of her husband Keith. Nothing brings her more joy than to meet and witness a widowed parent's growth as they rebuild the future for their family. These families are her inspiration.

Never did she dream that through tragedy she could find her gift to nurture hope in the families she supports.

🌐 www.hummingbirdcentreforhope.com
✉️ marny@hummingbirdcentreforhope.com
f HummingbirdCentreHope
📷 hummingbird_centre_for_hope
🐦 @HummingbrdHope

Without my village, there is no way that I would be where I am today. The list is too long to name everyone who has helped me in their amazing ways. I am grateful for every one of you, but most importantly my family—Dave, Scott, Taylor, and Nathan. The one person I want to thank, but can't, is Keith. Who knew what life would have for us when we met on the banks of the Bow River? Your life and death have taught me more and have made an impact on me in ways I never could have imagined. It's true what they say, "Love conquers all," and I carry your love with me for always.

She Is

Fierce

CHAPTER 13

RISING THROUGH THE DARK NIGHT OF THE SOUL

Kimberly Davis

It was loud, it was violent, and I was certain I would not make it out alive. I remember the smell of fire residue, and it burned my nose. I was running from them, and running fast. I found an abandoned house and proceeded up a winding stairwell that never seemed to end. As I ran up the stairwell to safety, I found a corner on the third floor to hide. Within minutes I could hear men talking, gunshots firing, and I knew I had to move once again. They wanted me, and they wanted me dead. I kept running—third floor, fourth floor, fifth floor, sixth floor—stopping on each to hide in a corner, only to find myself fleeing again. I soon realized there was no safe place, and I was going to die.

It was 1:15 a.m. when I woke up in the corner of my closet. My head was buried in my knees with my arms and hands protecting it, and I was rocking back and forth. It was just a dream, I told myself. This is just a dream. You have had these one hundred times before. It is okay. As I came to a clear woken state, I started repeating my mantra.

I am Loved. I am Safe. I am Grounded. I am Loved. I am Safe. I am Grounded.

I moved out of my closet and into the bathroom to take an Ativan to calm the panic attack. One milligram would do the trick. I climbed back in bed sweaty, anxiety stricken, and sleep deprived. I repeated my personal mantra over and over until I fell asleep. I am Loved. I am Grounded. I am Safe.

This dream would be one of many on repeat for years to come.

It was the summer of 1991 when my best friend (Jasmine) and I finished a long night of waitressing at a popular nightclub in our hometown. We were thrilled with the tips we had made and could not wait to go shopping. American clientele were our primary customers, and we were happy to receive their US dollars. The day after we worked, we decided to cross the border to go shopping in Detroit. Back in those days, most stores were closed on Sunday, but in Detroit, many stores remained open. We knew exactly what we wanted: white Coaster sneakers. They were cute, comfortable, and inexpensive. Payless Shoes was the place to purchase them, and this store was open on Sundays. Jasmine picked me up in her little red car and we headed to the border. Once we crossed the border, we drove downtown Detroit on Woodward Avenue until we found a store that looked open.

Fifteen minutes passed really fast, and before we knew it, we landed in Highland Park where the store was located. We pulled into the nearly empty parking lot and parked. I began to gather my things when I noticed that Jasmine was not moving. I looked at her and said, "What's wrong? Aren't we going in?" She said, "I don't like the look of those six guys walking toward us." I immediately felt anxiety well up inside me, and before we knew it, we were surrounded. A cold, hard, sawed-off shotgun touched my temple, and I watched my life flash before my eyes. The disbelief of what was happening left me paralyzed. My body felt like a rag doll. The pure beauty of innocence, my unwavering trust in humanity, shattered in a matter of minutes.

The fellow who held his gun to my head said, "Give me all your money and get the fuck out of the car." I reached down to grab my wallet and passed it to him through the open window. We were forcefully ushered out of the car and then one guy tried to push me into the back seat, but my head kept banging into the door frame. His buddy urged him to stop pushing me, saying,

"Come on, man, we don't need them. Let's just get the car and get the fuck out of here." The guy pushing me said, "No, these bitches are coming with us." The man who was petitioning his buddy not to take us was nicely dressed. I remember thinking he was handsome and wondering, "Why are you doing this?" I felt sick at the thought that I was assessing his physical appearance, but there was something about him that seemed different from the rest.

Ultimately, we were left standing alone in the parking lot. Neighbours were on their porches and people were hanging out around the street corner watching everything. Jasmine and I both started crying as we looked at one another and said, "What are we going to do?" Within minutes, a big gold Ford LTD came rolling up. Driving the car was a woman who had her two kids in the back seat, and she started yelling out the car window, "Get in, get in." We were so confused. Was she in on this thing? We did not know what to do. Then she said, "I'm going to help you. I saw the whole thing!" We decided to get into her vehicle, and she quickly drove away. It was frantic; she was frantic. She screamed, "I knew those motherfuckers were going after you. I have been sitting here watching them because I knew they were going to hit you girls. What are you doing in this part of town anyway?" My voice filled with tears, and I replied, "We were buying shoes."

The driver's name was Sadie, and she told us how this sort of thing happened all the time. She told us that there had been a dead man lying in her neighbourhood park for the past two days. She said, "I called the police, but they don't come to our neighbourhood."

I was sitting in the back seat with her two kids while the wind blew violently through the open car windows. Her children were smiling and so sweet. The young girl was about eight, and her little brother was maybe five years old. Both children had the biggest smiles ever, and with the sun beaming on their faces, they glowed like little angels. I felt held and safe with them. My heart ached at what they had already seen and for the grim possibility of what was to come of their lives. At that moment I felt so grateful for my life, and for just a few seconds, I forgot what had just transpired.

We arrived at a community police department and went inside to file a report. When we walked in the small community precinct, Sadie yelled out the details of what had happened. Several police officers looked our way while casually resuming their desk duties. Finally, an officer decided to talk to us and unconcernedly sauntered over.

After taking our report, he said he would call us for updates. As he walked away, I said, "Excuse me, can we please use your phone to call our parents?" He said, "There's a pay phone across the street." He turned his back to us and blithely walked away. We were in shock at his response. I said to him, "We don't have any money; we were just robbed!" Sadie reached in her pocket and gave us coins to use in the pay phone, and I called my father to pick us up. As my father pulled up to the station, we said our goodbyes and never saw Sadie again.

I wish I could have talked to Sadie again to thank her for her kindness and to repay her somehow.

That night when Jasmine and I got home, we both slept for the next couple days. By Tuesday, we were back at school. It was our graduation year, and everyone was busy thinking about prom and graduation. Our boyfriends supported us, as did our friends, but it was never really mentioned again. My parents rarely, if ever, brought the carjacking incident into conversation. I never went to a counsellor, and I essentially pushed the trauma down somewhere where I could not find it, until it found me.

I spent the next twenty years living and reliving the gun incident in my dreams. My dreams were consistently very dark and always involved violence of some sort. I developed hypnagogic hallucinations—"vivid visual, auditory, tactile, or even kinetic perceptions that, like sleep paralysis, occur during the transitions between wakefulness and REM sleep."[1] Many consider this phenomenon "a function of higher-order consciousness because it involves metacognition (the awareness and understanding of one's own thought process) in the form of reflective thought and attempted control of negative emotional impact from the dream itself."[2] While now I feel like it is a gift, during the years prior I could not accept it as a blessing or sign that I needed deep healing. The lucid dreams felt like a death sentence and perpetuated my suicidal thoughts.

I was always a fearful, deeply sensitive child. I was raised in an authoritarian home with a verbally and physically abusive stepfather and a mother who suffered from anxiety and depression. My mother rarely talked about her condition and suffered in silence. My stepfather shamed me for my sensitivity. At the early age of five years old, I was nicknamed "sucky baby" by him. He could not understand my sensitivity as it made him extremely uncomfortable, perhaps because he did not know how to connect with his own sensitivity and emotion. Showing emotion in my household was considered weakness unless it was rage or anger. Even still, we dared not stand up or express ourselves after my stepfather spoke. If so, we would be met by face slapping, punching, belts, or whatever accoutrements were available at the time to silence us.

My mom used to chase my stepdad around the kitchen with bleach when he was preparing meat because she feared we would contract salmonella from poor food prep. When we went out as a family, my stepdad would have to turn the car around, sometimes twice in one outing, to head back home because my mom always feared she left a candle burning, the stove on, or the curling iron plugged in. When we were driving behind a car and the person in front of us threw their cigarette out the window, my mom would cover her eyes and yell, "Tony, don't drive over it!" She feared our car would blow up if we drove over a lit cigarette. I recall one night when my parents were watching a TV program that featured a story on bed bugs and dust mites. My mom was so rattled by the story that she stripped all our beds that night and bleached the sheets in hot water. Bed bugs and dust mites became my new neurotic fear.

My mother never worked outside the home. She spent her days caring for her four children and her husband and maintained the home. It was a full-time job in every sense of the word. Every day she had a meal prepared for us, and the house was always spotless. There were days when she obsessively vacuumed the carpet and dusted the tables. Tubs and toilets were always cleaned. She cut the grass, took out the garbage, and walked to the grocery store and then carried five to six plastic bags home. She took us by bus to all our doctors' appointments when my stepdad went to work during the day. She was on top of everything and was a great mom, but she held so many secrets inside that haunted her life. My heart still aches when I think about it. When I look back on our lives, I see how much she suffered internally. I wish I could have helped her, and I miss her dearly.

After the carjacking incident, I found myself modelling much of her behaviour. Driving on the highway and seeing a cigarette fly out of the window from the car in front of me gave me extreme anxiety because I thought my car would blow up if I drove over it. When I visited my boyfriend at his house, I had to vacuum his couch before I sat on it. If I was unable to vacuum it, I placed a sheet on it before sitting down. Additionally, as soon as I arrived at his house, I found myself rushing into his bathroom to clean the toilet before I would use it. I'd dust the tables and vacuum his carpet. Only once these tasks were complete could I relax. This obsessive-compulsive behaviour lingered throughout my twenties and into my early thirties. It manifested into social phobias, racing thoughts, and repetitive behaviours.

I became obsessed with details. Unless I knew that every detail met my expectations, I could not complete anything. School was always a challenge for me, but I kept going. After high school, I studied at college for three years, then moved on to university. Constantly striving for perfection, I struggled to recall the material I studied. When I discussed my habits with my peers, it was obvious I studied longer and harder than most of them but could never level-up grade wise. My anxiety and fear-based thinking affected my performance. When I did make the "A" grade, the excitement only lasted for a few minutes before I moved on to my other per-ceived failures. I never felt worthy or good enough. My insecurity was debilitating at times, yet on the outside, no one could tell that I was living a life of quiet desperation.

The gun incident was an outward representation of what I was already feeling inside. Fear. Living in a household where my step-father was physically and verbally abusive, to experiencing extreme bullying in high school, I found myself suicidal. I never felt safe. I wanted to escape the constant feeling of fear—fear of death, fear of homelessness, fear of failure, fear of disease, fear of rejection, fear of loss, fear of physical injury. Just like my mom, I lived my whole life fearing everything, even myself. Suicidal ideation was common for me starting early in high school and lingering on to the rest of my life.

I felt so alone, scared, and hopeless. I hated who I was and that my body and mind felt so much. I felt as though I didn't fit in anywhere.

The years that came after the gun incident were marked with extreme social phobias and traumatic PTSD nightmares. While in university, I studied Psychology and Women's Studies. It was not until after my first year studying Psychology that I finally realized I needed professional help, and this help is where the unravelling started. For the first time in five years, I started talking about the gun incident and many of my childhood traumas. I was twenty-five when my psychologist diagnosed me with depression and generalized anxiety disorder. I knew I had suffered from these disorders my whole life and was deeply committed to my healing. I thought it would be a quick fix. Little did I know that I would spend the next twenty-four years in a pattern of reactivity, rage, fear, addiction, loss, and heartbreak.

Upon graduating university at twenty-seven years old, I entered a career in automotive manufacturing that, in many ways, mirrored the atmosphere of my childhood home. There was yelling, profanity, insensitivity, and fear. Emotions such as anger, competition, and frustration were acceptable, but when an individual displayed exhaustion or sadness, they were considered weak. Crying was an absolute no. In my business, crying was career suicide, especially for a woman. The culture was that of "The Old Boys' Club," laden with decades of patriarchal rule and sexism. It was an intense, dynamic environment that demanded I push down the truth of who I was if I was going to excel and survive. It was reminiscent of how my stepfather raised us.

Seemingly, everyone was there for one thing: money. This work environment was highly toxic and filled with animosity. When I shared my discontent about my career choice with my stepfather, he said, "Money talks, bullshit walks, kiddo." Company-leased cars, fancy vacations, nice homes, and beautiful clothing were the collateral for the abuse I took. People looked at me as if I had everything. I was always well put together and positive and generous with my time, money, and material possessions. But inside, I was slowly bleeding to death.

I continued to chase the dollar, not the dream.

I had the uncanny ability to adapt to any environment I was in. Living in the fight or flight response continued to be my life and my pulse. It was all my body and mind knew. I was constantly overworking, fighting with co-workers, and moving, and I rarely rested to recharge. My soul continually cried out, and I tried to bury it with just about everything I could find. I was addicted to working, shopping, travelling, drinking alcohol, and exercising. I would wake for work and end up in my garage skipping rope at 5:00 in the morning before busily getting ready for a ten-hour shift on my feet.

I would exercise again after work, then go home for dinner. I threw the best dinner parties, designed my own clothes, celebrated friends and family, and took the lead on anything and everything I could.

I always found time to obsessively shop. There were so many items in my closet that had price tags on them and were never worn. Nothing was ever good enough. I could not satisfy the hunger that perpetually lingered in me. The feeling was that of intense longing and discontent. I was on and off antidepressants and anti-anxiety medication, but nothing ever really helped me. I was married to the most amazing human being but still could not quell the internal suffering. I eventually lost my marriage, and to this day, it is one of the hardest things I have ever had to reconcile.

I continued to search outside myself for validation but could never shake the feeling that something was missing.

After seventeen years of service, I decided to take a promotion at a US facility with my same company. My plan was to retire after achieving twenty years seniority and do something I love. I felt excited to be starting over somewhere new and was finally feeling positive and hopeful. I was tired but believed I could do it. Almost twelve months into my new position, I knew I was going to have to leave sooner than I thought. My anxiety was at an all-time high, I was working long hours six to seven days a week, and I was slipping into a deep depression. I was drinking martinis every night after work to numb myself, then went to bed to start the same cycle over again, day after day after day.

While at work one Saturday afternoon, a colleague named Reggie approached me in a panic. He said, "Kimberly, there's a man in here with a gun." I immediately called my supervisor and told him to call security. I asked where the man was, and Reggie told me he was just outside the door. He said he was after his ex-girlfriend because she broke up with him. Within minutes, the gunman walked into the building and started heading toward us. My first instinct was to protect my people, so immediately, I evacuated more than fifty employees to a safe location. When I returned to the scene, police and security had still not arrived. By this time, the gunman had gone outside, and no one could find him. Then, as I walked around the area, he suddenly walked back inside the building. He had a bright satin San Francisco 49ers jacket on. His hand holding the gun was in his pocket, and I could clearly see the shape. He walked toward me, and I stood still. I stared at him in absolute awe that a gun situation was happening . . . again. But this time I was not scared. In that moment when we locked eyes, I was fearless. I felt strong and empowered. I believed that if it was my time to go, then so be it. Just shoot me, I thought to myself. Just shoot me.

Several employees appeared and called him over. They gathered around the gunman in a circle and told him that his girlfriend wanted to speak to him. One of the employees took out his phone, handed it to the gunman and said, "Here, use my phone to call her." When the gunman took his hand out of his pocket, the guys jumped on him. They took his 9mm Glock, disarmed it, then held him down until the police arrived and arrested him.

After completing a long police report, safety incident reports, conference calls, etc., I could go home.

I was back at work the following Monday, and it was business as usual. Only one member of my management team mentioned the incident. No one except my hourly employees asked how I was. I was the first person on the scene, made the initial call, and successfully evacuated my area on two separate occasions during the incident. I was given accolades on the shop floor for having handled the situation so well. In hindsight, I just wanted to hear my bosses say, "I'm glad you're okay. Is there anything you need?" I got over it quickly, just like I did the first time I was held at gunpoint. After all, it was the same packaging, just a different incident. Let us pretend it didn't happen. So that is what I did.

I have always been a seeker. Even during the biggest storms in my life, I have continued to search for deeper meaning and a connection to a Divine Source. My spirituality deepened in my mid- to late-thirties as I gradually began to understand the truth. I visited Buddhist temples in Thailand, climbed Machu Picchu, lived at an Ashram, obtained various yoga teacher training certifications, became an Ayurvedic Wellness Educator, obtained certifications in reiki and meditation, studied Thai yoga massage, and sat at the feet of supposed gurus. I filled my home with crystals, drank green juice, took ADHD medication, performed Pancha Karmas, and experienced spiritual response therapy (SRT) clearing, Chinese meridian clearing, and acupuncture. I saw Ayurvedic doctors and shamans. I had entities cleared from my subtle body and had all my chakras rebalanced.

I may have cleared some past lives by out-of-town shamans. I jumped out of planes in Wisconsin with my young lover and took long rides on Harley Davidsons. I regularly visited a social worker and psychologist. I had a couple good friends on speed dial who held space for my fearful rants. I slept with women and even had a few lesbian orgies. I got breast implants that I quickly regretted.

I went on an adult lifestyle website with the thought that maybe if I became involved in a threesome with a married couple that this might fix my loneliness. I regularly sat on my ex-husband's front porch, drinking wine while he lovingly held space for me. I went over the same stories again and again, hoping to leave with the answers to my problems.

Self-help became another addiction, another thing on my to-do list scheduled in on my calendar of what had to happen next for me to be "enough." I still came back to the same suffering and inner emptiness that plagued me my whole life.

Within the same time span, over an eight-year period, I watched both my parents die of cancer, lost my marriage and friendships, became estranged from my eldest sister, and lost my house, my career, and my savings. I stared down a gunman in my workplace, which triggered unhealed trauma from the carjacking when I was nineteen. I had a heartbreaking romantic relationship that started and ended abruptly, and I tried every medication and supplement I could to "fix myself."

Having these things occur was intense and left me questioning my capabilities and how I got myself into these circumstances. I could no longer rationalize why I was even here. My physical body was breaking down as I lived in extreme physical pain and chronic fatigue. The mysterious illness "fibromyalgia" showed up. I found myself unable to get out of bed or show up for anything or anyone, including myself. I was unable to climb five flights of stairs into my apartment without gasping for breath, I took the elevator at work, and I parked as close as I could to the front door.

I constantly cancelled on friends and lost thousands of dollars by not showing up for courses, workshops, events, etc. I did not know how to ask for help because I had so much shame. I was filled with profound anger, and my skin felt as though it was on fire every day. I was at a loss, and I wanted to die.

In 2018 I was diagnosed with complex post-traumatic stress disorder.

According to psychotherapist Peter Walker, complex post-traumatic stress disorder (C-PTSD) results from enduring complex trauma. For example, children who felt unwanted, unliked, rejected, hated and/or despised for a lengthy portion of their childhood may experience it. Often, trauma becomes deeply ingrained in a person's body, mind, and soul. While the origin of C-PTSD is most often associated with extended periods of physical and/or sexual abuse in childhood, many individuals who have endured repeated verbal and emotional abuse, prolonged workplace abuse, repetitive bullying, and emotional neglect also fall into this category of diagnosis.

Survivors with C-PTSD have an exceedingly difficult time with emotions—experiencing them, controlling them, and for many, just being able to comprehend or label them accurately. Many have unmanaged or persistent sadness, either explosive or inaccessible anger, and/or suicidal thoughts and extreme anxiety. Often labelled as "empaths," they are extremely sensitive to their environment and energetically to those around them.

Ten months into my third sick leave from work and feeling hopeless, I embarked on a three-week intensive mental health program that was life changing. Having studied psychology and in-depth spiritual studies for many years, I did not believe I could learn anything else that would help me. This belief was not the case. I dived deeply into C-PTSD from an allopathic standpoint and wove in my spiritual Ayurvedic studies to better understand what was going on within me. Living a life that is based on the teachings of Ayurveda and yoga has been pivotal in my healing.

The mind is cunning; habits and addictions are neural programs constantly running, as is our response to them. Thoughts are not real; they are just thoughts. I began to see how my thoughts affected my body and my life. Much of my life choices were based on trauma response and conditioning. I was responding to my body and the mind's quest to feel what it knew: anxiety. I was creating situations that invoked this response because anxiety felt like home. I was continually making self-sabotaging choices that perpetuated the self-loathing and helplessness I was feeling—choices that left me physically sick, remorseful, and fearful.

Although I came to this understanding, I could not take back what was already done. The Law of the Universe, "Cause and Effect," states that every action has a reaction. I had to live accepting the part I played in my messy life. This reality continues to be exceedingly difficult for me. There was one thing for sure; I could no longer do it alone, and coming to this conclusion and moving out of the victim mindset was a huge milestone for me.

I learned how to pray and surrender and discovered faith.

My life had been inviting me to wake the whole time. First, I had to accept death—the death of Kimberly as I knew her, who I thought she was and that of my other selves. I only change when I am forced to change, and therefore, I ignored the whispers of the Universe that told me I had to stop running. Those whispers soon became loud yelling, that soon became a powerful knock-down to a bottom of deep, dark discomfort. The shedding and letting go of all that was not me was inevitable, and next would be the rebirth and rising into the Universe of who I really am.

I have always casually taken the metamorphosis of a caterpillar to a butterfly. It has been somewhat of a clichéd story for most, but for me, it has been a profound metaphor of my life. To live through a metamorphosis like the butterfly, we must surrender everything.

The descent into darkness and identification with death was necessary for me to transform. Just as the butterfly must put itself back together from scratch, so did I. Healing is not a one-size-fits-all situation. It truly is a lifelong journey of death and rebirth as

r igation">
THE GREAT CANADIAN WOMAN

we gather wisdom and profound life lessons along the way.

I wish someone had told me that the only person who could take me through the Dark Night of the Soul was me. The only person who could make me feel safe and loved—was me. In all my resistance and in looking outside myself for happiness, the truth was already here inside me. I first had to allow surrender and stillness to enter my life and be willing to sit with all of it. I had to love myself just as I am. Going in search of myself as a goal was an illusion. You do not have to go anywhere to find peace. It is right here where you are now.

Hafiz said it better:
"You don't have to act crazy anymore—
We all know you were good at that,
Now retire, my dear,
From all that hard work you do
Of bringing pain to your sweet eyes and heart.
Look in a clear mountain mirror
See the beautiful ancient warrior
And the divine elements
You always carry inside
That infused this universe with sacred life
So long ago."

242

Kimberly Davis

Kimberly Davis was born and raised in Windsor, Ontario, where she has had a successful twenty-year career as a manager in automotive manufacturing. Kimberly now lives a life dedicated to the service of others in the practice, study, and teaching of Ayurveda and yoga. Kimberly is a passionate advocate for mental health awareness and is deeply committed to helping reduce the stigma associated with mental illness.

Kimberly has the innate ability to create harmony and lead with compassion and empathy. She is fiercely loyal and deeply intuitive, and she gives of her time and heart unconditionally to her friends and family. With unstoppable spirit, Kimberly has taken adversity and transformed it into meaningful experiences, not only for her own personal growth and development but also to help other women move through challenges that will support their journey to live a life of truth, connection, health, and well-being.

Kimberly knows first-hand that it takes persistence, patience, perseverance, and commitment to heal and change deep-rooted beliefs that often compromise an individual's ability to live a full, heart-centred life.

You can find Kimberly cooking beautiful, healthy Ayurvedic meals for friends and family and teaching the time-tested principles of following an Ayurvedic diet and lifestyle. She loves travelling, exercise, spending time in nature, reading and writing poetry, and visiting local art museums and theatre productions.

@shantipriya00

My story is dedicated to those whose lives have been touched by mental illness indirectly or directly. To those who have experienced suicidal thoughts, those who have lost loved ones to mental illness, and those whose lives have been touched by suicide in any way, this story is for you. In other words, this story is for all of us. To all the mental health workers, you are valued and needed.

Thank you to my family and friends who accept me as the unicorn I am and for your patience with my disappearing acts and many cancellations. To my girlfriends for believing in me when I could not believe in myself and for listening to my tireless ponderings of life and the deep stirrings of my heart. To my best friend and ex-husband, Philip Poli, for the countless evenings spent on your front porch holding sacred listening space. To those who gently held a mirror to me that led to deep self-reflection and healing.

Deep bows to the sacred practices of yoga, Ayurveda, and Buddhism that continue to be my foundation for living a heart-centred life based in truth, compassion, and continued personal growth.

She Is

——— Empowered

CHAPTER 14

BREAKTHROUGH

Trisha Doharty

Pain. Such a little word but one that has such a huge impact on how we function and make decisions in our lives. Pain creates a memory that becomes sensitive to certain stimuli that triggers a reaction, even if no real threat is present. That is what happens to our brain when we experience some form of trauma. My pain became such a norm in my life that, in turn, I became aware that I was reacting to something that didn't necessarily exist but rather is reflective of previous pain. This has been my life. I have been living reactively instead of in the present. My pain has a beginning that I often forget because it has been buried and hidden deep in my mind. Pain that has been collected through a series of events and experiences in life up until this point—events and experiences that weren't always my fault, but mine to manage and find a way to live with. This is a story of a young girl's journey into woman-hood, motherhood, self-discovery, and healing. This is my life.

My preteens were tough and confusing for me, and worrisome for the adults in my life. When I was eleven years old, something shifted. I did not feel as social as I once did. I felt withdrawn and quiet, and some may have chalked that up as just being shy. But it was more than simply being shy. I was troubled. My mood was all over the place. One day I would wake up feeling fine, and the next day I would lie crying in my bed all day. During this time, I said nothing to anyone. I didn't understand what I was feeling. I didn't understand why it was happening. I felt that a piece of me was broken and missing, but I just didn't know what it was. I think that not knowing how to express my feelings only deepened my emotional volatility, and my behaviour became just as erratic. I was fighting at school. I was not listening to my parents or my teachers. As a child, I couldn't understand my internal pain, and I couldn't place what triggered the deep sense of panic. I had no recollection of any trauma; I couldn't pinpoint exactly what caused me to begin to withdraw into myself. I felt like I was always caught up in my mind. I lived in my head because the real world was too much to digest, and I escaped it as much as I could.

When I was thirteen, I started seeing a boy. Technically, he was a man. He was eighteen. We had a great relationship—for a while. He listened. He was thoughtful. The time I spent with him made me feel normal again. I started spending all my time with him, and I felt safe with him at such a young age because he respected my wish that I was not ready to engage in sexual activities. Until he didn't. I was sixteen when he assaulted me. He assaulted me because I wasn't ready to have sex with him. I had no idea it was coming. There were no red flags, no warning shots, no alerts. Nothing. I couldn't understand it. I fought back, but I was shaking in my soul. I just couldn't understand why a simple disagreement would lead to something so damaging. So violent. So violating. My *first* wasn't romantic, sweet, or respectful. It was traumatic. I was left feeling vulnerable and questioning my worth. You never expect or plan to be betrayed by the person who is supposed to love and care about you. It took me a couple days to process what had happened. I finally broke down and cried. I cried because a part of me knew that it was not going to be the last time. I cried because I felt violated. I cried because the first person I loved took everything from me. I cried because I couldn't tell anyone; I couldn't even tell my parents because I wasn't supposed to be dating. I wasn't taught about abusive relationships, what they looked like, or what the warning signs were. I didn't know what to do.

Being sixteen, I still didn't fully understand what had happened. I thought that if I apologized, things would be okay and would go back to being how they were before. I thought that if I gave him what he wanted, he would be calmer, and we could get back to having fun. It was difficult. I was always on guard because I had no idea what would set him off. I was scared that an attack would happen again, and I lived so fearfully and became so critical of the things I said and did that I started to lose myself. Trisha was no longer Trisha. I just felt like a body that was physically present but was mentally, spiritually, and emotionally withdrawn. All over again. The physical and sexual assaults eventually stopped, but they were simply traded in for psychological and emotional warfare. He became manipulative, selfish, and verbally abusive, and he never shied away from telling me everything that was wrong with me. I started hating myself. My self-esteem was shot. Everything I did was criticized. I wanted so badly for it to end. Our relationship didn't help the depression I had carried with me from my childhood, and it just became worse over time. I was great at pretending everything was good when I was around people, and so I held it all in. I needed an out but just could not figure out how to get one.

I was nineteen by the time the opportunity to leave presented itself. I went to Jamaica for a vacation to see my mother and decided to stay there for a while. The agreement with my mom was that I could stay if I got a job or attended university. She had no idea what I had been going through, and I couldn't bring myself to tell her. So, university it was. I chose to study psychology. I figured that it would help me learn all the tips and tricks I needed to heal myself from the torment that was in my mind. I just needed an ounce of reassurance that I could help myself and move on. During my studies, I tried to find myself and start rebuilding, but it didn't go as expected. I was too unstable from the abuse, and the path that I was on was so rocky that I really started to spiral. I thought I needed attention to help fill the void in my heart, and I sought it in a very damaging way. I found myself attaching to people who were just as harmful as the last. They manipulated and used me, and because I felt so frustrated, helpless, and powerless, I lashed out at everyone in my path. It was like I thought because I was hurt that I needed to hurt other people too so I wouldn't be alone in my pain. I had no love for myself, and I had no idea how to get the love and care that my soul yearned for. I was lost. So lost.

One afternoon at the age of twenty, I was crying on the phone with a friend, and she said to me, "It takes strength, determination, and bravery to overcome the obstacles that are placed before you. When the will to survive is stronger than the pain of letting go, you are going to sometimes wonder 'Why do I silently suffer when I know I can do better?'" Her words hit me, and I could feel my Soul regain some hope. There was a spark. It was small, but it was there. I knew I had to address my trauma, and I naïvely thought that with a background in psychology, I'd be able to "help" myself through my depression and anxiety on my own. It turns out that when you mix self-help with a refusal to accept help, it's a recipe for disaster. I couldn't bring myself to tell anyone what I had endured, so I kept it bottled up and buried, building up the internal pressure with each day that passed. I was a ticking time bomb waiting to go off, and I knew that whatever was coming would be damaging.

And I was right. Things took a bad turn when I attempted to self-harm. I thought that if I felt physical pain that it would give me an escape from the mental pain. I remember picking up a glass and squeezing it with rage until it broke. I then picked up a shard and squeezed it until it sliced into my palm. The temporary relief from my inner turmoil was euphoric. The wound in my hand became my new therapist, and when I needed relief, I would open it back up again. Truthfully, I don't know what was worse: the physical pain or the sheer fact that I was finding pleasure in hurting myself. It was time to ask for help. I mustered up the courage to see the counsellor on campus. That's what they're there for, right? Ha. Well, not only was she dismissive of my momentary act of courage in reaching out for help, but she wrote me a prescription that I was left to research on my own. I was shocked to find out she had prescribed me some very strong antipsychotic drugs. Antipsychotic drugs? I wasn't psychotic! I was hurting! It's like something within me started to suddenly fight for me, and I called my doctor back in Canada and told him what I had been prescribed. He was also shocked and told me not to take them as they would cause more harm than good to my mental health. I never went back to that counsellor, and once again, I found myself left to my own means to try and heal my wounds. I felt everyone around me had failed me, including my own self. I couldn't understand why it was so hard to just love the person I saw staring back at me in the mirror. I couldn't fight my mind to see the woman that was beautiful, creative, intelligent, and caring. Why could this version of me not settle in my mind? Why did I find myself to be so complicated? I overthought everything—nothing was black and white or taken at face value. I replayed every single conversation I had had with someone, trying to pick it apart and find some hidden meaning in what they had said, no matter how simple it was. My insecurities and lack of trust only caused more strain on my relationships with friends and loved ones. I made everything more complicated than it needed to be, and it made for a very lonely way of life, especially for a woman in her early twenties who should have been out enjoying her younger years.

After I finished my degree, that oh-so-helpful psychology degree, I moved back to Canada and went right back to the only thing I knew: the abusive relationship I had left behind. I assumed that being apart for a few years would do us good, as we had had the time to explore with other people. I needed to know if it was worth walking away from something I had invested years in, and inside, I just really hoped that the person I fell in love with as a young teen was still there. I tried to be "stable" while still trying to figure myself out. I tried to act normal, like there wasn't a raging fire inside of me every day. It didn't last long. I became unsettled and felt like I needed more chaos back in my life, like I wasn't already living with enough of it inside. I stepped outside of my toxic relationship and started dating someone else. It was fun, it made me feel alive, and it made me feel wanted. Desired. I knew what I was doing was wrong, but I did not want to stop. It's funny how life works—it always has a way of putting the wrong things to an end when you won't do it yourself. For me, that was an unplanned and unexpected pregnancy. I could barely take care of myself, so how was I supposed to raise a child? I cried for three weeks straight. It wasn't because I didn't want to be a mother, it was because I knew the hard road that was already in front of me just got a whole lot harder, and I was going to have to do it alone. It was just me, this precious child in my womb, and my internal chaos on this journey now. How do you think this story is going to go with my track record up until this point?

I tried my best during my pregnancy to use the energy I had to prepare for this little bundle of joy. I wanted it to work so badly, and I focused on keeping myself healthy and calm throughout the duration of my pregnancy so I could deliver a happy and healthy baby. You know how sometimes substance-addicted women get clean when they get pregnant only to relapse after the child is born? (Almost like watering a plant to help it grow while the roots continue to rot beneath the surface?) That was me, only I wasn't addicted to drugs or alcohol. As soon as my baby girl was born, the health and wellness I had built up during my pregnancy went hurling out the window, and I sunk into the deepest, darkest depression to date. Postpartum depression. How could I bond with this beautiful child if I couldn't even connect to myself? I loved her so much, but I couldn't bring myself to connect to her.

How could I not feel attached to a child that came from my own body? I couldn't even get out of bed for my beautiful baby girl. What the hell was wrong with me? What kind of mother was I? I was overwhelmed by everything and desperate to escape my own reality. What had I become? And how? Thankfully, my stepmother was with me, and she stepped in and took care of my baby while I tried to get my mind together. What a blessing. I was not ready for this role of motherhood. While my stepmother cared for my child, I wallowed in self-pity. I remember one day looking at my baby and asking God why she was given to me. I wanted her to be loved, but it felt like I didn't have any love to give. My mother (back in Jamaica), God bless her heart, was always encouraging me, praying for me, and just always speaking life over me and my baby. She was not there physically, but she was such a huge support emotionally and spiritually. She was my warrior when I felt like I could not fight anymore, and she never gave up on me even when I was tempted to give up on myself. My mother just kept breathing life into me, conversation after conversation. I knew I could be doing better, and after one particular call with Mom, I realized I was not fighting for just me anymore. I had a family that needed me, and I had to set better examples for my daughter. I thought of a way out, and it led to me moving to a whole new city. I escaped once again.

So, there we were, just my daughter and me living in a new city. I was twenty-six and didn't know a soul. Oddly enough, not knowing anyone in the city felt like the change I needed. It gave me space. It encouraged my sense of independence. It was the catalyst of getting my life together for the greater good of my child . . . and me. I felt a renewed sense of hope that this transition was the start of good things to come in my life. I left all the baggage and memories behind and looked forward to finally feeling that I belonged somewhere and could rebuild. I got a job, stayed under the radar, and tried to be a good mother, all while doing my graduate program. When it became a struggle to manage all the moving parts in my life, I made a conscious decision to be a stay-at-home mom and finish school. I finished my program with the uncertainty of whether I still wanted to be in that field because I grew to develop a love-hate relationship with counselling and psychology in general. It opened many wounds that I chose not to address, and it ripped the lid off the repressed memories I wish had stayed hidden. Ironically enough, with unhealed wounds (gaping, actually), I landed my first "big-girl" job as a group facilitator. And little did I know then, it would be a catalyst for my own healing as well.

Working as a group facilitator was eye opening to say the least. It was like someone was holding up a giant mirror with me standing in front of it, looking at all my own demons staring back at me through the eyes of these courageous participants. If I was going to lead these people through their own healing, I was going to have to do the hard work on myself too. I had to practice what I was preaching. Through this awareness, I developed my own program for myself as a way to work through my trauma and to start the healing process yet again. I knew that I needed to be completely honest with myself in order for me to have a fighting chance at my own trauma recovery. I had to dig deep within myself to find the strength I knew I'd need to tackle my painful truths. I had to be ready mentally, emotionally, and physically because I knew it was not going to be easy—it was going to be a heavy load to work through. The scariest part was knowing that I had very minimal support to help me when life became too heavy or too painful. With that reality, I went on a mission to find a support group that I could rely on emotionally.

Who knew a Facebook group would hold the answers? Through it I met Dana Fong-Aiu. She was so inspirational, and she completely captivated me. She hosted a challenge in the group, and it was empowering to see women come together and be vulnerable and honest while trying to build up themselves and their businesses. We had to create videos speaking to some aspect of our lives, and I spoke about the trauma I had experienced with my partner and how I was starting all over again. I was honest in stating that I just didn't know how. I allowed myself to be vulnerable, and the response was overwhelming. I was in awe of how supportive a group of women around the world I have never met could actually care about me and what I was going through. I felt like I was home among these women. I started seeing how my mindset was shifting in a positive way and how differently I saw myself. I had purpose. I had value. I was starting to rebuild the relationship with the Trisha I knew was in me all along. I noticed that the more I listened to my intuition, the more I started trusting myself. There was a cycle. A pattern. One that I was eager to keep repeating.

I was on a journey to self-discovery, all because an online community of women accepted me and my shit. Who knew?! There were no judgments. Somehow, I knew that my potential was bigger than my fear. I listed all the reasons why I felt like I could not do anything more than what I was doing, and they helped me to counter this list with all the reasons why I could. I felt it. I understood it. I felt something inside me was starting to shift, and I felt uncomfortable in my own body. I was emerging. I volunteered on some boards for non-profit companies, I did behind-the-scenes work with an amazing women's organization, I participated in some panel discussions about mental health and stigma, and I felt another shift. I felt like I was getting into alignment with something, but I just did not know what at the time. Somewhere deep inside I knew I was destined for so much more, and it kept me hanging on.

I knew I had a lot of hard work ahead of me, and to say that the next steps were easy would be a straight-up lie. My healing journey was not an overnight process. I still struggled to find my footing in the world, but for the first time I felt like I was at least moving in the right direction. I had so many ideas! I felt empowered. I wanted to trust myself to start something that I was passionate about, but it is said that starting is the hardest part—and it's true. I loved tea. I could start a tea business! I loved poetry, mainly because of how poetry allowed me to express myself in ways I was unable to verbalize when I was in pain. I could teach a poetry-writing class! I thought about ways I could help women in my community and how I could connect mothers with women from whom they wanted to learn. From these ideas, I planned and planned and planned as if planning were going out of style, and I wrote everything down, but I just couldn't seem to get any of my ideas off the ground.

Feeling a little discouraged, I decided to get a job so that I could build some sort of a social network and keep myself engaged. But all getting a job ended up doing was provide me with more of an excuse not to get started on building something of my own. I used my job as a reason to stall my dreams, even going so far as to take extra shifts just so that I would only have enough time to care for my daughter and sleep. Therefore, I could justify why I was not doing what I needed to do for myself. It was self-sabotage at its finest. I was fighting with myself because a part of me was ready to crawl out of my black hole for good and crush my goals, while the other part just wanted to forget about her ambitions, roll over, and die. I needed to be held accountable for my bullshit, so I reached out to Dana again as I knew she would keep it real with me. She listened to what I had to say and to all of my excuses yet again. She asked me to search within myself and see who was there: a weak-willed little girl or a warrior goddess? I knew I was more than competent, but if I could not believe in myself, how could I expect anyone else to believe in me? I felt ashamed. I felt silly because I knew I could do better for myself and for others, but I just couldn't get out of my head and out of my own way long enough to see it through. There was something in me that believed I wasn't worth the work, the dedication, and the fierce level of honesty that I deserved. What a trip. I had the highs of hope and the ideas for what's possible mixed with the lows of self-loathing and fear. And still, I kept fighting.

I knew the work. I help other people with the work! It was my turn. I remembered the workbook I had created for myself to work on my mental health, and I gave it an honest shot. I followed the work, page for page. I did the exercises, I journaled, and I cried. I opened up with myself and let some truths sink in. I forgave myself for a lot of things. At times it felt more emotionally taxing than the trauma itself, but I kept trying. *Just keep holding on, Trisha.*

I started to feel alive again and found a renewed sense of hope deeper than I had felt before. I was ready to walk into my light and lift myself up. I now knew my patterns and cycles, and this knowledge helped me better prepare myself for the inevitable lows. I got another new job and met some incredible people. My boss was amazing and very approachable. My team made going to work enjoyable, and I was doing something that allowed me to see the results in the people I was helping. I felt like my life was starting to be on the right path and that my purpose was coming to me. My eyes were opening to the life all around me, and I began to see every day how women just like me face disadvantages because of circumstances they likely never asked for. I could feel these women because I am these women. And suddenly it all began to make sense. My soul was yearning to help and to create a space for these women who just needed someone to see them in the same way I needed someone to see me.

I started a federal non-profit organization called The WISE (Women Inspiring Sisterhood and Empowerment) Initiative and began creating an online community of women who I could inspire and uplift. My goal was to create a space for mothers who wanted to get out of their current situation to connect with other women who were doing what they aspired to do. I wanted to bridge that gap and provide a safe space for women to learn from and empower each other. I wanted to provide easier access to the resources they needed to assist in improving their lives. Through this initiative I started meeting some really great women with amazing stories of strength and resiliency. I also listened to the horror stories they had to share. And much like my very first job of group counselling, the feeling of trying to heal these women while I was still hurting inside became distressing. I could not fight the anxiety that came back this time. The burden of trying to help others while not addressing my own issues led to a breakdown.

I had panic attack after panic attack because I felt dishonest. I was telling women how to fix their situations in order to start them on their healing journeys, but I was not doing the same for myself. I was choosing to ignore my own trauma, and as a result, I was letting my past continue to influence my present. And now, on top of every other horrendous emotion, I was filled with guilt. Enough was enough.

I needed therapy. I stopped being stubborn in thinking I could help myself, and I spoke to someone who I trusted and was willing to be honest with. I shared my fears over getting into a committed relationship again. I shared my fears about raising a daughter in this world. I shared about my lack of trust in people, and I shared about my fear of failing and why this new organization meant so much to me. I shared why I felt called to guide women on their journeys to be the absolute best version of themselves, and I shared that there were women in my past who I hurt by my actions and why doing right by this new organization is my penance. I shared all the big dreams and visions that were in my head and how I knew that I was going to make some kind of difference. I shared and I shared and I shared. It was like a purge of everything I had been holding in so tightly. I got on the right medications to help balance my brain, even out my anxiety, and alleviate some of the pressure I was placing on myself. As a form of therapeutic release, I posted about my recent experience online, and some people were compassionate and empathetic while others distanced themselves for their own reasons. But you know what? I was okay with that. I knew the journey I was on required the support of real people who had my back, and lo and behold, I found myself making even more genuine connections because of my openness and ability to be genuine myself by focusing on making connections that would impact my life in a positive way. I let go of things and people that were not serving me. I allowed myself to take breaks from the world as needed, and most importantly, I started becoming the example my little girl deserved so that one day she, too, will know how to navigate this tough world. I am solely responsible for what I put in front of her and the messages I am giving her. She needs to know that it is okay to ask for help when she is struggling, and that life is not always going to work the way we want, but if we stand true to our beliefs and the good we know we can do in the world, then all will work itself out.

Throughout this thirty-one-year process, the accumulation of my pain and damaging patterns taught me so much. I learned that taking time off is not only good but also necessary. That asking for help is not a sign of weakness but a show of true strength. I have also learned that as much knowledge as I may have, there is still more to learn. I now know that being open and honest with your family will reveal who supports you and who does not. I know that my daughter and I would not have been where we are today if it was not for the kindness of friends who have become family and family who remained consistent in their support of me. I have a lot of work ahead of me as I pave the way for the next generation of women who will bring about change into this world. I cannot wait to see the way The WISE Initiative will help bring about this change. To know that something I created from pain can and will have a lasting impact makes the journey to get here worth it. It was bitter, it was golden, and it was hard, but it also blossomed. It created a stronger version of myself. I haven't felt so close to being free in a long time, and I know it is coming. The journey will continue long after this chapter is closed.

Trisha Doharty

Trisha Doharty (she/her) is a mother, entrepreneur, mentor, coach, and friend. Trisha uses her experiences in life to bring change to her lineage as she raises a daughter who is curious, sensitive, caring, and wants to change the world. As such, Trisha created a legacy for her daughter so that she can learn from her mother's experiences. When she is not busy working, she is running her non-profit, **The WISE Initiative**, an inclusive space for all womxn and youth who are looking to improve their lives on a social and financial level. As a woman, Trisha believes in the upliftment and growth of women and aims to use her platform to speak on issues facing all women. Trisha has her master's degree in Clinical and Forensic Psychology and uses this to help those in the marginalized community who are often less thought of. As a previous Housing Stability Worker, Trisha has had encounters with those who sleep rough, have mental health issues, and struggle with maintaining housing. This drives her desire to build her community and the people within it. Trisha believes that all people deserve the basics of life and as such aims to bridge that barrier. Trisha is also a champion for her people and brings awareness to issues affecting the Black community.

f thewiseinitiative and tdoharty

⊙ @trishadoharty

⊙ @thewiseinitiative

I would like to thank my daughter, Haleigh, for always motivating me and helping me to grow. My dear girl, you will change the world! Stay wild, my love. My mother for all her encouragement and love. My father for always telling me to follow my heart, my siblings for pushing me to be the best version of myself, and my friends who have supported me through the hard days and loved me through it all. To Lauren Schefter who has been a second mom to my child on days I could not even breathe and is an incredible support system, THANK YOU!

Special Acknowledgment: To all the moms who feel like you are doing this alone, you are not. To the special moms in my life raising their babies and going through school, working, building business, all of the above, I see you, I feel you, I am you. I made it through and you will too. Chantel, Carolyn, and all the other moms, I am so immensely proud of you.

She Is

—————— Curious

CHAPTER 15

MY UNBECOMING

Lisa Di Domenico

As I lay in bed, tears running down my face and overwhelmed by defeat and sadness, I noticed her two-year-old little face poke through the door of my dark bedroom. Olivia looked at me and said, "Not again, Mom" with such heart-wrenching sadness and frustration in her voice.

My heart shattered even more than it already was. My daughter desperately wanted her mom. In fact, she needed me. However, I simply was not showing up in her life like she needed me to or how I wanted to. Drowning in the overwhelm that had become my life, I simply had nothing left to give. I felt guilty. I felt like a bad mom. I felt like a bad wife for leaving my husband with the entirety of the responsibility of caring for our family when I was just too drained to function, which had become most days. I hated how I was—*or was not*—showing up for my family, the people who mattered most in my life. I hated that I was modelling to my daughter everything I did *not* want to teach her. In that moment, I hated myself.

Once the emotions subsided and I stopped feeling sorry for myself, I kept hearing my daughter's words replaying in my head: "Not again, Mom." Up until this point in my life, the only person my decisions ever really made an impact on was me. But now my daughter was becoming collateral damage. In fact, my entire family was becoming collateral damage.

Being a mom is by far the most important role in my life. I have never wanted more for someone else than I do as a mother. I wanted to be everything Olivia needed me to be, and so much more. However, I began to realize that I couldn't be who she needed me to be if I wasn't well. That's when it clicked. If I wanted to be the mom Olivia needed and deserved, I had to be well with myself first—physically, emotionally, and psychologically. I realized that I would never be able to show up powerfully in her life if I couldn't show up in that same way in my own.

This realization marked the beginning of a new chapter in my life. It marked the onset of my journey of learning to listen to myself and to trust my inner "knowings." It was the catalyst to me breaking free from all the ingrained beliefs and practices I carried about what it meant to function and live in society and was the birthplace of radical self-acceptance and self-love. This realization marked the beginning of my unbecoming.

The day after hearing my daughter's words, I took myself to a walk-in clinic and was immediately put on a leave of absence from work. Diagnosis: burnout, depression, and anxiety. What a cocktail! I would be lying to you if I told you that I didn't know how I got to this point, because I did. That little voice inside me that would surface now and again and ask, "Is this it? Is this life?", that voice I was stuffing away deep down because acknowledging it created too much discomfort, it knew. Heck, I knew it knew. But it was easier to ignore it. At least it was in the moment, but I ended up paying for it later. It's kind of like not paying your credit card bill. The bill will keep coming, and while you can choose to pretend it's not there, there will come a point where you will have to pay it and it will be with interest. I definitely paid with interest.

Unfortunately, this wasn't the first time I went on a medical leave for burnout and mental health reasons, but how I spent this time was radically different from before. The first time I was ridden with shame, embarrassment, and guilt. I spent most of my time in a state of tremendous anxiety and navigating severe bouts of depression. I spent months looking like a rat stuck in a cage, furiously trying to find an escape route to avoid having to deal with my inner world. I just wanted a solution, and fast! The discomfort of my own existence at that time was torture—so much so that I contemplated ending my life to escape the suffering.

But this time, I didn't want to run. I was tired of running. I was tired of the emotional roller coaster that had become my life. I wanted off the damn ride, and I knew that the only way out was in. That day I made a very conscious decision to relinquish my ego and not let shame and guilt consume me by focusing on my why: my daughter. I committed to myself and spent the next seven months trying to understand where I went wrong. Hindsight is always 20/20, but in the moment, it was like moving through a hurricane: my world was spinning, and I couldn't see two feet in front of me. I could not understand where I went wrong in life. I did everything "right." I did everything I was *supposed* to do to live a happy and successful life: I worked hard in school, went to university, got a good job, married my best friend, and had a happy and healthy family. From the outside looking in, I had a life that so many would dream of having, really. So, why was I so unhappy?

Healing started and the answers began to surface when I reconnected with that nagging voice inside me, the one that had started out whispering that I was made for more but was now screaming for attention. When I started to listen, this is what I realized: What I felt I *should* be doing and what I *needed* and *wanted* to be doing were radically different. I had spent the last ten years of my life trying to fit a square peg into a round hole, forcing myself to conform to some sort of acceptable societal norm of what it meant to work and live a life that just did not fit with *who* I am, *what* I believe in, *how* I wanted to help others, and the lifestyle I wanted and *needed* to lead a happy, fulfilled, and purposeful life. Going against the grain for so long had literally made me sick—repeatedly.

I was living on autopilot and going through the motions. One unintentional step at a time, I was drowning out the voice within me that had been trying to tell me that I was going the wrong way. I did it because what it was telling me scared me. At some level I knew it was right, but I chose not to listen because I was plagued by fear: fear of change, fear of the unknown, fear of leaving a "good" job, fear of making a mistake, fear of failure, and fear of what people would think of me. So, for years, I let my fears win, and I settled. I quieted the voice and convinced myself that I needed to continue living the way that I was. I convinced myself that I just needed better coping mechanisms to prevent burnout. I convinced myself that I could not find better work and that I should be grateful for what I have. I convinced myself that my dreams and visions were just that: dreams and visions. I convinced myself to stay in my "comfort zone" because ultimately, I didn't believe in myself.

I grew resentful, angry, and cynical. I began to feel *trapped* and *stuck* in my own life. My mental and physical health began to suffer. My mental and emotional energy was being siphoned faster than any self-care regimen could refuel it. My life was completely out of balance and out of alignment. *The worst part?* The people I cared about most—my family—were the ones being most affected by my choices. *The irony?* I was settling because I had convinced myself that this was what was best for my family.

Thanks to my then-two-year-old, I realized I had it all backwards.

I needed to prioritize myself to be a better person and example for my daughter. I could not be a better, happier, and healthier person without honestly acknowledging what *wasn't* working for me in my career and life. Once I did, I knew that if things were going to change—*and they needed to*—I had to make different choices. I needed to make choices that honoured *who I am, what I value,* and *how I wanted to show up* in this life. I would have to make choices that took me out of my comfort zone. I would have to make choices that scared the crap out of me. But at this point, the discomfort of staying in my comfort zone had grown greater than the anticipated discomfort of leaving it. Now, the greatest fear I had was a fear of regret.

I feared modelling the exact life I desperately did not want my daughter to aspire to, which is what I had been doing up until this point. I feared what would happen to my marriage if I continued to live the way I had been living: chronically unhappy, anxious, and depressed. I feared spending a large part of my life doing work that did not feel purposeful and meaningful to me, at the expense of my wellness, and all for the purpose of paying bills. I feared looking back on my life and regretting not having followed my heart and listened to what I knew would be best for myself, my family, and my career. I feared looking back on my life only to realize that I always existed but never really lived. Instead, I wanted to know that I didn't settle for less than I deserved but strived to be all that I could be and more. I wanted to know that I did everything in my capacity to create a fulfilling and purposeful life so that I could look back on it with nothing but feelings of contentment and satisfaction. I wanted to be able to look back on my life and know that I offered the best example I possibly could to my daughter about what it means to be a woman, a mom, a worker, a partner, and a friend. I want to show her what it means to love and accept herself fully and give her permission to trust herself and follow her dreams even if they scare her or don't make sense to others. In order to do this, I needed to embody this.

Figuring out what I had to do, while not easy, was the easy part. Actually doing it was one of the hardest things I have ever done in my entire life. You know how in the pupa stage of a butterfly's life cycle the caterpillar essentially decomposes in its cocoon before it transforms into a beautiful butterfly? That is the most accurate way I can think of to depict what the change I had to go through was like. From the outside, it looks like nothing is happening, but on the inside, there is a total and painful yet spectacular transformation occurring. There is a death of sorts taking place—the death of a version of myself that I no longer wanted to be and the emerging of the person I was always destined to become. It's what my inner knowing was trying to tell me all along. It knew.

While there are numerous discoveries and lessons I learned about myself throughout that process, there are a couple personal truths that were particularly challenging yet life changing. The first truth I had to accept was that I did not love myself. There were so many parts of myself that I spent my entire life trying to deny, minimize, or hide, parts that I grew ashamed of and that in my mind's eye made me flawed. What I perceived to be my greatest flaw was my sensitivity. Let's face it; society isn't kind to sensitive people, especially sensitive women. We are perceived as emotional, out of control, and even hysterical at times. I had accepted that being a sensitive and emotional person was a bad thing. I carried that with me. I believed it. I despised this about myself. But you know what? When I reconnected to this part of myself, I recognized that my sensitivity is also what makes me a darn good helper and mom. I see, feel, and sense things, subtle things, that people miss all the time. My emotional perceptiveness is what allows me to create deep connections with others. It is this connection that makes me able to both understand and help people in the way that I do. In denying my sensitivity, I was not only causing myself to suffer, but I was denying my gift and my purpose, and continuing to deny it meant continuing to reject the essence of who I am. There is no way happiness can live in that space.

I decided to redefine my relationship with my sensitivity and embrace it. In changing my relationship with this part of myself, I was able to shift my self-perception. In turn, this shift made it possible for me to love and honour all of me. In doing so, what others thought about my sensitivity no longer mattered because I knew its potential and understood its purpose. I knew that in denying my sensitivity, I was also denying my gift, my purpose, and my happiness, and I was just no longer willing to do that for the comfort and approval of others. They didn't need to understand it. They didn't need to understand *me*. I didn't need their approval. I was *finally* standing in my power. My sensitive, messy, vulnerable power. The weight of the world had lifted.

This shift led me to uncovering another personal truth about how I had been showing up in the world—a truth that was so hard to admit and accept because it went in complete contradiction to the belief I had of myself. I had been playing the victim. Writing those words is still hard. I had been blaming others and circumstances for my frustration and unhappiness for as long as I could remember. I perceived everything that went wrong in my life as happening *to* me. I perceived myself as helpless to my own circumstances. I blamed others for how I felt. Looking back, it makes sense that I would behave in this way because it allowed me to keep denying the part of myself that I despised—my sensitivity—and deflected away from me having to take responsibility for my unhappiness. What I didn't realize at the moment is that by behaving this way, I was *choosing* my unhappiness every single day. Blaming others and circumstances left me powerless over my own life because as long as everything was everyone and everything else's fault, I could do nothing about it. As long as I continued to perceive life in that way, I was putting myself in a place of helplessness. As long as I waited for others or circumstances to change, I was miserable. Acknowledging and accepting that I was the reason I was so unhappy was one of the hardest personal truths I had to overcome throughout my process of healing and growth. It meant that all my pain and suffering over the past years was MY fault. That realization took me on a roller coaster of shame, embarrassment, sadness, guilt, anger, frustration—you name it! But then, it liberated me in ways I could have never imagined. If I was the cause of my unhappiness, it meant I had the power to now change it. So, I did.

I began putting the pieces of my life back together again. I did it very intentionally with honesty and vulnerability. I began to deconstruct my belief systems and teachings and replaced them with ideas and practices that honoured my true self, my purpose, and my life priorities. I began to shift my mindset and perception to one that fostered my emotional and psychological well-being. I took action to create the career and life I needed to live purposefully and authentically. In other words, I was unbecoming.

In our society, selfishness is a bad word. It's seen as a blatant disregard for others and their feelings. I disagree. When done with intention, selfishness is one of the greatest gifts you can give yourself and others. In being selfish, I am better able to be *selfless*. Paradoxically, in taking care of myself and nurturing all that I am,

I show up more powerfully in the lives of others. In investing in my wellness and my happiness, I am a better mom, wife, helper, and friend.

So now, I choose selfishness. Now, I choose me first. I choose to honour myself every single day. I choose to show myself the same love and compassion I show others. I choose my purpose even when others don't understand it. For the first time in my life, I trust and listen to my inner knowing because I know it's guiding me on the right path. For the first time in my life, I stand in my power and know that I am enough. I am the only person who needs to love me and understand my life choices. I am the creator of my own destiny. I am the creator of my own happiness. Understanding and harnessing this power has not only changed how I work but has also changed how I mother. It has changed the partner I am to my husband and the person I am to my family and friends, and it has completely altered who and what I attract into my life. While we think of responsibility as something that can sometimes feel heavy, taking full, unwavering, radical responsibility for all that I am and am not has ironically made life so much easier to navigate. When you stand in your power, confidence follows. Confidence makes decisions easier, choices clearer, emotions steady, and trust flow.

Today, I relish in the liberation, relief, and peace that comes with knowing that I am enough. When challenges arise, self-doubt creeps up, and insecurity manifests, causing me to question myself and my journey, I recall how this journey started in the first place. I go back to that pivotal moment in my mind, picture my daughter's face in the doorway of my dark bedroom, and I respond, "Never again, Olivia" and persevere. I persevere because now, both my children are watching.

Lisa Di Domenico

Lisa Di Domenico is a career coach and mental health advocate. When she is not helping others become the best version of themselves and create an aligned life, you can find her indulging in life's simple pleasures with her husband and two children.

Unsatisfied with the frameworks available to her to practice in her industry, Lisa spent years searching for a way to have a greater positive impact on the lives of others while being able to maintain her own well-being so she could be fully present for the people who mattered most in her life: her family. Leveraging her university education in psychology, ten years' experience as a certified guidance counsellor, as well as her own personal growth journey, Lisa decided to create the professional "container" she had been longing for by making a career transition toward coaching and founding her business ***Lisa D—Life by Design™***.

Lisa is best known for her drive, passion, perseverance, and devotion to helping and advocating for others as it relates to personal growth, mental health, and wellness. She is recognized for her ability to effectively and efficiently assess the needs of others as well as her authentic, empathic, and direct approach in guiding and supporting others in achieving their professional, personal, and life goals. Lisa believes that our purpose is found where our personal and professional lives align, and this is what she strives to help others achieve.

🌐 www.lisadlifebydesign.com

📷 @lisa_d_lifebydesign

📘 lisadlifebydesign

💼 lisa-d-life-by-design-inc

To my husband who has always believed in me even when I didn't believe in myself, thank you for being my best friend, my number-one fan, and for your constant and unwavering support in the pursuit of my crazy ideas and dreams. You have been a pillar on my journey, and I feel truly blessed that I get to share my life with you. To my children, Olivia and Noah, because of you and for you, I have grown into a person I never thought I could become. You have taught me resilience, courage, vulnerability, self-trust, and self-love. It is through these lessons and because of them that I am where I am today. I am incredibly grateful and proud to be your mom.

She Is

Inspiring

CHAPTER 16

MY PURSUIT TO FULFILMENT

Peggy Birr

I had my son at fourteen years old. Yes, fourteen years old, long before it was cool. As a teen mom, I could have very easily fallen into a life that looked very different from the one I currently live. In fact, that may have been easier in many ways.

Living in a small rural town, I heard the whispers, the comments. I felt the change in people when they spoke to me, while others simply avoided me like the plague. I felt the glares and stares as I walked the hallways at school, the grocery stores, the neighbourhood. I went out, but only when I thought I wouldn't see anyone so I could avoid the feelings those encounters created.

I endured so many judgments from others. Even those in presumed positions of authority voiced their negative opinions and thoughts, throwing them around behind my back or directly at me. I distinctly remember a teacher, YES, a teacher, who told me I would not amount to much. I would love to talk to her now because now I have the words I didn't have then.

We, as humans, need to realize how our words may land and make an impact on others. Words can cut deep and tear down. Words can also lift, inspire, and support others. Words can make people feel seen and heard. Words can make people smile, or they can make people cry. The words spoken to me during my teen pregnancy affected me, some in good ways, but others cut deeply.

I endured the names and the social shame that circulated around being a pregnant teen. Some people were very good at slapping their judgments on me, and those judgments did cut deeply. As a teen mom already having a vulnerable state of mind, it would have been very easy to give in to the opinions of others. Easy to believe what they said to be true. Easy to fall into a victim state of mind. Easy to fall victim to systems and the environment around me. I had never known anyone who had ever lived this life experience. I only knew what I heard society around me say about teen moms, and many of those things were not positive or kind.

I could have continued to hide like I had my pregnancy for almost seven months. I became very good at hiding, blending into the background, not ruffling any feathers. That is what I knew. I think I found a form of security in that. What I can tell you, however, is that hiding becomes lonely.

But I chose differently. I chose to thrive, I chose to be somebody

I was proud of, and I chose to prove them all wrong—good or bad in that thought. I proved that their negative thoughts and their selfish, nasty comments did not get to decide my outcome. They did not get to shame me and keep me hidden.

Years later, I realized that even though I put on a very stubborn front about not giving a shit about what people thought or had to say about me, I actually did. I cared. I wanted to be liked. I wanted to fit in. I wanted to be seen and heard (who doesn't?), but at the same time, I didn't. And yet, while this pregnancy was one of the most challenging times in my life, I wouldn't change it for the world. It gave me my son, and it helped shape who I am today.

My pregnancy was only a piece of the puzzle that is my life. I grew up in a home that had love, but that word was not spoken often. There was some fun, and there are some good memories. There was also chaos, confusion, and arguments. Lots of arguments. The root problem to all the arguments, as I remember, was money. Always money. I have a parent who has a gambling addiction, a sneaky addiction that, like all addictions, eats away and erodes a family. It erodes relationships and the feeling of security.

Was life horrible? No. Was life calm and filled with one happy moment to the next? No. It often felt hard, and I always felt like I was walking on eggshells in my own home.

With all this chaos in my life, I grew up as a people pleaser, a very perfect little people pleaser. I am also the middle of three daughters, so if you are a middle child, you know what I am saying!

Growing up, I was referred to as Switzerland, as in "neutral." I was very good at not rocking the boat, not ruffling feathers, not giving anyone reason to get angry. I was good at keeping the peace. I was the quiet, shy kid, the good kid, the one who never caused a problem or trouble. I was the one who was always scanning the environment around me for any problem and then I would set out to fix it to make it more comfortable for all, to make it better somehow.

I built a thick wall around myself and my heart, and very few people were allowed in there. The problem, however, is when you have built a wall around your heart, it not only keeps out the bad feelings but also keeps out the good ones. I am still working on tearing down that wall all these years later. The self-awareness I have gained through doing A LOT of personal development has allowed me to realize that the wall I built protected me from many things. It helped me be who I am today; it helped me survive some very challenging life experiences. Perhaps it is because of that wall that I stand here today and am not lost in a broken system. However, as I healed through my personal-development journey, I saw that the wall was no longer serving me. As I said, when you put up a wall to keep out the bad, it also keeps out the good.

Letting go is not something that comes easily to me. I have been called stubborn, and I have a very proud side, but at no time will you hear me say I am perfect! I know that I'm not a teen mom anymore; I also know there are parts of that time that I still carry with me. I was fortunate to have had two parents, despite their own issues, that supported the shit out of me. Even though they didn't say it much while I was growing up, I know they are proud of me. I know many women in similar circumstances do not have or did not have the support they need or needed. I send all of you so much love.

With a lot of grit, stubborn determination, family support, and a teacher who went above and beyond her duties (Ms. Davidson), I completed my grade nine high school year. You have heard the saying that you have to celebrate yourself, right? Well, I celebrated that I went on to finish high school and achieved top marks in some classes. I also received more than one award plus bursaries at commencement time. I went on to post-secondary education, supporting myself through and personally funding nursing school and became the first and only one in my family to graduate high school and college. Achievement is something I know well, and I didn't mind working my ass off to get it.

I always thought nursing was how I was meant to help other people, and for years, it has been. Currently, nursing still is a part of my work, but five or six years ago, I hit an emotional, exhausted, burned-out wall—a concrete wall of unfulfillment and feeling like something was missing—and all that started a shift. I was shocked, never thinking that feeling unsatisfied and unfulfilled in my career would happen to me. It took me a long time to admit this unfulfillment to myself, like years. Admitting it made me feel like a failure, like I had a character flaw, and certainly not perfect. Remember the people pleaser, the perfectionist?

I was feeling unfulfilled in a profession I had loved for many years. I started to resent going into work every shift. I hated feeling that way, and I hated feeling alone in that feeling. I did not want to admit it because it would seem like a failure, but I was burned out. Years of shift work, years of nursing, and years of people pleasing had caught up to me. I was becoming bitter and resentful on the inside because—god forbid—anyone knew things weren't perfect! I also felt shame around these thoughts and feelings. Who was I to feel like this? My life was pretty damn good. I had a loving husband and three incredible kids, I travelled and had vacations, and I experienced many of life's blessings. I had so much more than others and so many things others wish they had, and here I was feeling like something was missing. And I felt so guilty and ashamed for a long time for wanting more. My lack of fulfilment and resentment spilled over into all areas of my life, disrupting my inner peace. How could it not? There was a place in me where my fire had dimmed to an ember.

I was frustrated, resentful, bitter, angry, and disconnected on the inside, especially at work. These feelings I had been holding inside started to show up on the outside during every shift. They were easily feeding into the negativity around me and adding to the loneliness. I honestly asked myself, Is this it? Is this how it is going to feel from now until I retire? Is this some "midlife" crisis?

Retirement for me at that time was ten-plus years away; I could not imagine the scenario of feeling that way at work for another ten years. I did not want to live that scenario. I needed a solution. I needed it ASAP. What I was doing was not working.

It would have been "easy" to just try and survive. I could have tried to make it to retirement without starting my business because one thing I have learned is that this shit is hard. I could have just put up with my job and continued, hoping for the best for the last ten years or so.

I also could not imagine that scenario.

I knew something had to change. I searched for something different, another way to earn an income, a job that would light me up again. However, I was forty-four years old, so I could have chosen not to bother. But I realized that I might not survive emotionally if I continued on with the way I felt. So, with that knowledge, I created change. That change led me to a passion I would have never found if I had just kept doing what I was doing, feeling like I was feeling, and hoping to survive while I did it. I waited a very, very long time for others to change things, and for the things around me to change. Guess what? Things never changed! You know why? Because it was ME who had to change! I WAS the common denominator. How scary yet empowering that concept was.

The discomfort of waiting for others to change how I was feeling, waiting for others to create the change I craved, finally became painful enough that I went in search of something different. I searched for a solution to my problems instead of continuing to wait—instead of becoming another statistic to burnout. I assumed what I was experiencing was burnout, as I had been at this game for a long time. Nursing is stressful; shift work is stressful; life is stressful; people pleasing is stressful. I did not want to be "that nurse"—the nurse no one wanted to work with; the nurse with the toxic energy and attitude.

I finally understood that by waiting for others to create the change I craved, I had wasted precious time. It kept me feeling stuck, and it kept me feeling frustrated and feeling like I was spinning my wheels. I saw a glimpse of the personal power I had. I began to understand I had always had this power, all along! During all that time I had been waiting, I actually had the power I thought "they" had. By waiting and relying on others to change things, I had been giving my power away, and I did it for far too long.

By living a life catering to everyone else, by giving everyone my all, I had put myself in a dangerous position. That position? The bottom of my own priority list, the absolute last place any one of us should be. I, like so many other women, thought in order to be a "good" mom, a "good" spouse/partner, a "good" friend, a "good" employee, a "good" whatever, I had to look after everyone else first. By catering to everyone else, we effectively put ourselves on the back burner or, I dare say, remove ourselves from the stove completely. This was me.

As I reflect on my journey, I see that this behaviour was born out of the way I was raised, the things I saw, and the things I heard. It was born from a society around me that accepts and encourages women to run themselves into the ground for everyone else and praises them for doing so. At the same time, it judges the women who may take a moment for themselves and makes them feel guilty for doing it. No one bats an eye when women juggle a million balls at a time, trying their hardest to keep them all in the air yet feeling like a failure and all alone in this daily struggle as they do it.

When I went in search of something different, the change I thought would be the answer was the creation of another stream of income—the creation of an income from home so that I could leave nursing because it felt that bad, that much like something was missing. I no longer wanted to work shifts or holidays, and I did not want anyone telling me when I was allowed to take vacation or for how many days I could be gone. Most of all, I wanted to feel in control of my own day and my own life.

I ended up in the world of network marketing. I had no idea there was this other way to make an income! But what I really fell into was the world of personal development. For that, I am forever grateful. I had zero idea what the words *personal development* even meant or what it was. Most of all, I had no idea about how it was about to change my life in ways I never imagined or ever dreamed.

In this new world of entrepreneurship, I found mentors and role models I admired. You see, my circle was and is very small. No one around me was "into" personal development. In fact, I was made fun of for trying to create a more positive environment, and in the end, I actually lost friendships over it. I had to look to podcasts, books, and online and in-person events. I followed accounts of those I admired and respected for guidance and support. I looked at these people as role models, people who felt and lived a life how I wanted to live. I wondered what they were all doing, how they got to where they were, and how they went through their days.

One thing I found they all had in common was that they all had morning routines! Thus, I started to evaluate how I started my days. For me, I would hit the ground running like my hair was on fire. Guess how my day went? Yes, the same way. The morning practices of my mentors set up their day for success. They started and created their day with intention. The concept of a morning routine was something I had never heard of, but it was certainly something I needed. Could it work for me? I figured it was worth a try; after all, what I had been doing wasn't working.

I started implementing a morning routine, a practice of taking time for myself, quietly, setting up my day with intention and positivity—yes, positivity. This routine has become a solid, non-negotiable one in my life. I have seen and, more importantly, felt the difference this routine makes in my day and my life, not only for me but for those around me. I added an evening "wind-down" routine, and most importantly, I started implementing boundaries, which I quickly learned I never had. No wonder I was exhausted! I looked at how I had been managing expectations, and I started being kinder, more compassionate, more loving, and less critical of myself. It was a game changer.

All this being said, it does not mean I do not have hard days. Things aren't all rainbows and unicorns over here, but I now have the tools to get me through the rough times with more ease and more kindness toward myself and those around me. Self-development is a continuous work in progress; it is a lifelong journey.

I see now how ridiculous it was of me to wait for others to create the change I wanted and how outrageous it was for me to expect others to be responsible for something like my happiness, joy, and fulfilment level. No wonder I continued to feel like I did for so long. But finally, I stopped waiting and started doing, taking steps to propel me toward the life I craved. I attended women's events (places where I felt uncomfortable), so I could grow. I put myself in the vicinity of other women with whom I resonated: women who encouraged me, cheered me on, and saw me for who I really was. I wanted to stop feeling alone in my struggle, despite being surrounded by people, despite having a loving husband and three awesome children.

Now, six years later, and after much self-reflection and personal growth, I realize I am here for more. I am here to empower other women who find themselves feeling like I did: exhausted, fed up, frustrated, and alone, not feeling good enough and like something is missing, and praying for a solution to end the perpetual cycle of chaos, self-sacrifice, and lack of fulfilment. I am here to guide them and to show them they are not alone and that they have the power to transform their lives. They have the power to live a life they are obsessed with, despite how they currently feel.

IT IS POSSIBLE.

I see so many women sacrificing themselves so they can look after all those around them, fit in work, and juggle all the things. I know this routine very well; remember the people pleaser I talked about earlier? Women too often believe it is wrong to put themselves first—that they can't possibly take time for themselves because it would mean taking away from those they love and care about: their kids, their spouse/partner, their family. They feel guilty even thinking about it.

I am here to tell all women that taking time for you absolutely benefits those you love. Taking care of you first allows you to be fully present, more energetic, and loving when you're with those you care about most. The ones you worry and care about will thank you for doing so later. You want your loved ones to get the best of you, not the rest of you, which is what my kids often had growing up. You do not know how much I wish I had known then what I know now about self-care and boundaries and how they completely change your day, your week, your life.

My goal and the reason I am here (besides taking care of damage already done while in the ER) is to empower women to care for themselves first and to show them how to have the most energetic, vibrant life they truly crave—a life they are obsessed with—and to tell them that they deserve to feel their best every frigging day.

I want you to close your eyes; yes, close your eyes. NOW imagine IF you lived the life you crave, a life you are obsessed with. What word comes to mind as you picture that life? How does that feel?

This is how The Fulfilment Project started: with me knowing I had to share what I learned, what I had experienced, and how it changed my life. The Fulfilment Project started as a community for nurses, but I quickly realized I was leaving behind so many women. I believe so many women are silently suffering in the chaos and overwhelm, feeling like they are failing and are alone in it all, so I opened it up to a larger community in order to empower and make an impact on even more women.

In September 2019 I hosted my first women's retreat. I have now created a mentorship program, The Fulfilment Formula, where I empower and guide women to reclaim their personal power and elevate their lives. The program is designed to empower women to own their day and their life, and to end the perpetual cycle of chaos, self-sacrifice, and exhaustion. It guides them in implementing self-care and self-love practices, guilt free. It encourages them to love themselves. I am passionate about changing the global mindset about how women think of, love, and accept themselves and society's beliefs and expectations of women in this world. I want women to live a life they are obsessed with, and to do it ALL without guilt.

I KNOW that when one woman changes her life, it changes the lives of those around her. What starts as a drop turns into a ripple of change and gradually creates a wave that travels farther than she ever imagined. One drop becomes a wave. One woman turns into many. One habit becomes a life.

I am tired of and frustrated by watching so many women struggle to get through their days, then falling into bed at night while feeling like a failure because their impossible "to-do" list didn't get done. They compare themselves to others who seem to have it all together (News Flash: they don't!). I am tired of seeing women run themselves into the ground unnecessarily just to love on other people, and I'm tired of seeing that they (and society) do not see it as a problem and deem it okay to do.

It is not okay, ladies. It does not have to be this way.

I currently still work in the ER, but because of all the work and personal growth I have done, I have been able to change my perspective. I set very clear boundaries with myself in regards to work and my schedule, something I had never done in the past. One massive decision I made after becoming clear on my values and evaluating my priorities and my joy list was that I changed my position at work. I went to a casual position, something I had been thinking about for a few years but never did. Why? Because my identity was tied to a title and an income. I worried about others' opinions and was afraid of the unknown.

One of the best things I ever did for myself was move myself from the bottom of my priority list to the top, front, and centre. I am hell-bent on showing other women how to do the same. Women need to not merely survive but thrive; to not only live a life they are obsessed with but to show up as their best self in this world and for those they love. Women need to show up as ALL of them, not as a part of them. This passion fuels me when I wake up, and it brings a spark back into my life. It has not only been my biggest adventure personally but also my biggest and steepest learning curve. I would not be able to guide anyone if I hadn't first had my own journey of finding more joy and fulfilment—a journey that continues today. It is a lifelong journey.

My journey has been a roller coaster, diving deeply into the stuff I had avoided for years. It is a journey I started for ME first. However, despite my kids being young adults now, they are still watching and learning from me. I never want to see them at the bottom of their priority list. I am here to show up for them and for you; I am here to show them/you how important they/you are; I am here to show them/you what is possible. Knowing my kids are watching propels me forward and keeps me going, even when it is hard. For me and for them, I continue to keep myself at the top of my priority list. I am no longer hanging out at the bottom waiting for leftover time—time that never arrives.

I had zero boundaries in my life, which (to no surprise) hurled me toward the wall I hit. I was at everyone else's beck and call; I catered to everyone else first. I also work in a profession where I literally care for others all day long, a profession that encourages nurses to put themselves last and is a constant source of self-sacrifice if you let it be. And many nurses let it be, something I know because I was one of the nurses who let the job dictate my life.

I wish I'd known these things when I started out in life, in the working world, and in the world of motherhood. Our education system does a huge injustice to us by never teaching us these principles and practices.

I could have continued to "survive" somehow until retirement, maybe. When your knowledge is cardiogenic shock, traumas, heart attacks, and broken bones—and you have zero business knowledge—entrepreneurship is a whole other world. When you are really good at what you've done for many years and then start back at ground zero, it feels like a mountain bigger than most. But feeling shitty and not having the life and choice freedom I craved was even harder. As a mentor of mine always said, "We get to choose our hard." That advice was a game changer for me. Having a mentor was a game changer. I did not do all this change alone, and I don't think many can. I needed guidance, support, and accountability, and that's where mentors and coaches came in. So now I am here, navigating a whole new world as someone who is fifty, despite the sideway looks I receive, despite the blank stares I get when someone asks about my passion, and despite the sometimes hurtful comments. My WHY for continuing to climb this mountain, even when I doubt myself, is simply that I cannot ignore a world that expects and accepts women to sacrifice themselves continuously while calling it caring and loving behaviour. I want to see a global shift in that thinking.

I would love for you to take away a couple of my lessons and save yourself the time and frustration that I felt. Move yourself from the bottom of your priority list and place yourself up top, front, and centre, and stay there. You are meant to thrive, not just survive, in this life.

I waited an enormous amount of time for others to change the things I wanted changed. I learned I was waiting on the wrong person. It was ME who had the power to change things. When we wait for others to change our life, we give away all our personal power. How ridiculous is that?

YOU have the power to create the change you crave—the change you have been waiting for—and you've always had that power. It just has been buried a little in the hustle and chaos of life. If I can create the change I have and venture out on this epic adventure, then you can too! Whatever your dream is, however bold your passion, YOU have the power.

You can do it. Isn't it at least worth the try? What IF it all worked out like you hoped? Or better?

Peggy Birr

Peggy Birr is known for her love of travel, hiking, camping, and being at beaches and in the mountains. If she isn't doing one of those activities, you will find her cuddling her grandbabies. You may also find her racing Ontario's bushes and trails with her spouse, John, in adventure races. Peggy is known for her infectious energy, and her humour will keep you in stitches as she is the self-proclaimed "Kramer" of the crowd.

Peggy has been a nurse for more than twenty-nine years, most of which time has been spent in the ER. Peggy always felt this job was how she could help others. By living every day like it was an emergency with chaos and self-sacrifice, Peggy hit a wall twenty-five years into her career and knew something had to change. After her own journey to create the change and positive impact in her life, she recognized that many other women were at risk of hitting the same wall of feeling unfulfilled and frustrated. This realization helped her understand the areas where women needed help in changing their lives. She wants every woman to live their most fulfilled life; a life they are obsessed with. This passion is her zone of genius: she guides women to thrive, not just survive, every day, and to care for their overall wellness including mind, body, and soul. Peggy is a women's empowerment coach, a self-care–self-love advocate, and your very own cheerleader!

Inspiring, empowering, positive, supportive, strong, advocate, forward thinker, friendly, and approachable are just a few of the descriptive words you will hear from others when they speak about Peggy. Past clients say she has a heart of gold.

With Peggy's guidance, her clients have transformed their lives, stating that they feel comfortable sharing their challenges and that they appreciate a different perspective that helps them see things from a different viewpoint. They are incredibly grateful for having worked with her.

Peggy is here to make an impact far beyond the ER doors. She is here to have women move themselves up their priority list, guilt free. Her passion is to change the global mindset on how women think of and love themselves. Changing her own thoughts completely shifted Peggy's life, and now she guides women to do the same through The Fulfilment Project community and The Fulfilment Formula Mentorship program.

📷 @peggybirr

f facebook.com/groups/fulfilmentproject/

🌐 peggbirr.com

John, most of what I do would never be possible without you, my wingman, my life partner, my best friend. You always support me in every idea I dream up and every challenge I face. If you aren't walking beside me, you are out in front leading the way, and if you aren't out front, you are behind me, supporting, encouraging, and pushing me along.

Jeff, Trista, and Emily, my three awesome children, the ones who are always watching, thank you for being not only my biggest teachers but a constant source of joy and inspiration. I am so proud to be your mom. My two grandbabies, Hudson and Molly (and the one on the way that I can't wait to meet), you have shown me I can love more and that I can certainly love bigger.

And Dad, who isn't here to see this or read it, thank you for the lessons.

Lastly, I thank you, my braver self, the self that raises her hand and says yes before the other self has a chance to get in the way. Without you, these words would not be written.

She Is

——— Brave

CHAPTER 17

I AM A LIGHTHOUSE

Jane Middlehurst

This isn't the chapter I originally wrote but a completely new one, written at the eleventh hour in our publishing timelines, literally down to the wire. The change came at a really interesting time in my life, as all things like this do.

I was recently in therapy after a really difficult time within my family. The first time I walked into my therapist's office, I half-jokingly said, "I'm here to deal with family stuff—you know, because it's all them and definitely not me." Sometimes, you've just got to lighten the load with laughter because I knew, of course, I was there to do some deep and healing inner work on myself.

Well, therapy week two should've come with a warning that went something like this: Jane, this week will be a shitshow. There will be lots of crying big hot tears—not quite an ugly cry but almost. You're going to feel like the wind has been knocked out of your sails, like that punched-in-the-gut feeling you get when the roller coaster drops. That's going to happen a lot this week. Whatever comes up, feel your feelings. Write about them too.

Of course, a warning like that could accompany any therapy week, but on this particular week I was raw and reeling from some big revelations in therapy about childhood trauma and the passing of my mum.

Later that same week I received a message from the lead author (Jackie VanderLinden) of this book. Originally, my chapter was written for a different book in *The Great Canadian Woman* book series, but long story short, it was to be moved over to this book, and while a lot of my original chapter still fit, Jackie had something to say.

I first met Jackie six months ago on a group call where we exchanged our stories, so when Jackie reviewed my original chapter, she felt so much of my story was left out. We got on a new call and she said, "I know you have a deeper story in you; don't you want to share that?" I knew exactly what she meant because people like us sometimes still dance around our losses, but I knew she was nudging me to include the loss of my mum in my story. "Jane, do you want to write your chapter all over?"

Yes.

I feel like it's times like these when you look back and realize that things come together for a reason. The book had been selected.

My chapter was written, done, closed. But then a bunch of things came together like little messengers all nudging me to share my deeper story with you, because there is healing in owning and sharing our stories, and when you share your story, you not only heal yourself but you help others heal too.

MOTHERLESS DAUGHTER

I am a motherless daughter. Saying this phrase feels like an important part of owning my story because for most of my life I've held this fact at a distance because, well, it happened so long ago. I was eight years old when my mum lost her almost-five-year battle with ovarian cancer. Every time I think of her battle, I know for sure that she gave everything in her to be with us as long as possible. Warrior. Mama Bear.

My life has been divided into the *before* and *after* of her passing. I don't have a lot of memories from the *before*, but some really stand out vividly, like:

Her baking a merry-go-round-themed cake for a school bake-off, complete with animal crackers for the carousel horses

Her painting the eye back on my Cabbage Patch Kid that had worn off

Her asking me about my second-grade crush

Her planning amazing kid-party activities

Me asking her to spell the word "always," and me being confused that the letter *a* could be in a word twice

Her telling me that she would never see me get married, and me being confused about that

Her sitting me down at the top of the stairs and gently trying to tell me that she was sick, and me not understanding why that felt so heavy

The day my mum died I was eating Kraft Dinner in the family room with my brother, sister, the neighbour, and her daughter. The neighbour was babysitting us while my dad was at the hospital with my mum. When my dad came home from the hospital that day, my brother, sister, and I went to the living room where my dad, grandparents, my mum's best friend, and maybe a few others had gathered to wait for us. I can still feel the thickening atmosphere of that moment collecting in my throat as I type these words now. I can still see the look on all their faces. A pin could have dropped. And then my dad said, "Mummy died today." The moment was awful. And then I went back to my Kraft Dinner. The neighbour's little three-year-old daughter asked me what was wrong and why I was crying. I told her my mum had died, and she asked what that meant. I didn't know what to say because I don't think I even knew what that would mean for me.

THE VISIBLE AND INVISIBLE

The death of my mum has always been the thing that happened to me in my childhood. This big traumatic event easily overshadowed the things that *didn't* happen, the more subtle things that hung out in the background of my childhood like the fact that no one really talked about my mum. Why did it feel okay for her to be in picture frames around our house but not okay to talk about her?

One time, my dad gave me Wynonna Judd's first album and there was a song on it that reminded him of my mum. I could see how emotional he was, and I loved him for that. I listened to the album on repeat, totally loving it, and this is when I started singing. Music was a life saver. Still, why do I remember feeling alone for so much of my childhood? I felt completely different, lost, and sad, like no one could possibly ever understand. Why did I swing alone at the park for hours every day while listening to music with no one ever checking in on me? There were times when I was in therapy, yes, but I'm talking about every other adult in my world—how come no one asked me how I was doing? I don't remember being in an atmosphere where we talked about my mum freely and openly or ever talking about my feelings or being encouraged to express what was on my heart. And yet, I can see how my dad was grieving and how maybe other adults found it difficult to bring up my mum, knowing it would be painful to speak her name. Maybe they just assumed that someone else in my life was checking in on me. I see all perspectives more clearly now, but in my formative years, I was simply a child without her mother.

Losing my mum was the visible event that happened in my childhood—my big pain point and my deepest wound. But it took me well into my adulthood to realize that there were also invisible things too—the things that didn't happen—that also shaped me.

It can be so hard to see the things that didn't happen because they can go by unnoticed. An event that happened can easily overshadow things that didn't happen.

TOO SENSITIVE

No one ever told me that I was too sensitive about the death of my mum, but I did hear quite often in my childhood that I was "too sensitive" in general. People would say, "You're being too sensitive" or "Oh, you know, she's sensitive . . . always deep in thought." I remember a story my aunt told me about a distant relative who met me only once and told her that I was different, special in some way. I asked what that meant, but my aunt didn't know.

Most often, being "too sensitive" felt like something to hide away so that it didn't get in the way. There were times when being too sensitive made me feel ridiculed, embarrassed, small, and silent.

It wasn't that the death of my mum made me a highly sensitive person because I have memories of being sensitive even before she died. However, the way my world shifted after she was gone laid some early groundwork for struggles that a sensitive person like me can have when they don't know who they are, how to care for their needs, or how to use their voice.

As a kid, I tried to minimize and repress my sensitive needs. In turn, my sensitive side began facing the outer world and the people in it, allowing me to sense people's needs, have empathy for others, pick up on subtle energy when someone walks in a room, notice a mood shift, intuitively sense things beyond words and body language, know exactly what someone is feeling, and tune into others.

In the first part of my life, I didn't know what it meant to be sensitive and how to care for myself. I didn't know being sensitive could be anything other than a burden. To the little girl who is "too sensitive" for the world, life can be challenging to navigate. The reality of life will shape you, but in return, that deep sensitivity allows you to shape your life in beautiful ways. It allows you to explore who you are with compassion, and it gives you insight into what makes you, you.

LIFE LEAVES LITTLE CLUES

As it turns out, being a highly intuitive and sensitive person has some real gifts. As the years unfolded into adulthood, I saw glimpses of how being a highly sensitive person attuned me to the world around me. It felt like having a sixth sense, giving me access to deeper sensing, deeper knowing, and deeper connection with others.

Where it once felt like being sensitive was a weakness to be hidden, I now began noticing that my sensitivity was actually quite powerful. It happened small and slow at first in the form of everyday conversations with colleagues and friends. It was just so natural for me to tune into someone's inner world and sense so much about them intuitively. It was like I was looking out into the world through their eyes, their heart, and their experience, and picking up on little things.

It wasn't me who initially noticed that there was something different about me. It's often the people in our world who help us see ourselves more clearly. Not noticing that something is different about yourself is especially true when it comes to your gifts because although your gifts have been with you all along, it's also the reason why they can be so easily overlooked by you. I call this the "gift blind spot."

Sometimes, these intuitive "sensings" and "knowings" came through so strong and so fast that I just went with them without question or hesitation. The fear of being wrong was outweighed by my boldness. So, I took a chance and began sharing what I was sensing. At first, I felt wobbly and unsure, like I'd die of embarrassment if I was wrong, but over time, I learned to trust myself, lean into my intuition more confidently, and just let her fly.

I discovered that the more I trusted my intuitive senses, the more other people felt seen and understood. Seeing and understanding someone automatically brings qualities of humanness, compassion, and empathy, and it can open the door of possibility to brave new worlds. In those moments, our walls soften and melt away. We disarm instantly when we are seen and understood because there's nothing left to protect. It was in these tender moments where I found an opening, a catalyst moment in the making, and the birthplace of possibility.

In my professional career as a corporate learning and development professional and leadership coach, there were more little clues showing up about how being a highly intuitive-sensitive person changed my work, deepened my connections, and altered how I just generally showed up. The curious clue-like thing is that I heard people consistently describe me as a natural coach and a catalyst.

Catalyst: *an event or person causing a change.*

I started paying attention to what being a catalyst might mean as it related to me and in my work. Whenever I felt like I was in the midst of a catalyst moment, I began to "live" this very question: *What do I notice about myself in this "catalyst" moment and how I'm showing up in it that contribute to it being a catalyst moment?* Because as you can likely relate from your own lived experience, people in your world use specific words to describe you and these words are little clues that can help you uncover your gifts. Part of our human experience is to gather those clues and connect the dots to find the unique intersection of our gifts and expressions.

In the corporate world, I noticed that I was able to pick up on and sense things in conversations with others; I was able to do it at a larger scale. For example, I was able to intuitively understand groups, understand difficulties within a situation, spot patterns, sense unspoken truths, and see the real story.

I didn't know that this "catalyst" thing was even a thing. I didn't know it was a unique, transformative superpower. Notice what comes effortlessly and naturally to you. These are your gifts. These are the things that other people admire and desire in you. These are the things that draw people to you. Looking back on my life there was always this intuitive, sensing side of me that picked up on everything. Imagine if we all embraced and honoured our unique ways of taking in the world around us—the different information centres: cognitive, sensing, somatic. Or more simply put—the head, heart, body. What if we embraced the whole human?

For most of my life, I struggled with the pain and pleasure of being an intuitive, sensitive person. Life was really challenging sometimes, and other times it was pretty darn magical. What we often resist though, is that our greatest gift lies next to our deepest wounds. Look where the pain is; what do you protect? What is most sensitive to you? What do you care fiercely about? What comes naturally? What do you honour deeply? Therein lies your gift.

ENTERING THE WOUND—THE AGE SHE WAS

This is the part that feels really vulnerable and brave to share. A lot happened the year I turned thirty-seven, which is the same age my mum was when she passed. I quit my corporate job. I was awakening spiritually. My life got more intentional and meaningful in so many ways. The pace of life slowed down. My focus shifted inwards. And my "mom stuff" also came up.

Of course, I saw none of it coming, but I also wasn't surprised by it either. As the poet Rumi said, "The wound is the place where the light enters you," and so wouldn't it be so fitting that my thirty-seventh year of life would be the year to kick off a big transformation?[1] It feels like something written in the stars. So, trust the timing of your life.

"The healer's gift is her own wound. It's the source and true understanding of compassion and forgiving. To heal thyself, embrace your wound as your sacred teacher." - Brooke Lillith.

The mysterious process of metamorphosis is that the caterpillar doesn't know what the darkness of the cocoon holds, but still, she trusts. Some caterpillars resist the process of spinning their chrysalis until the following spring, postponing their transformation by a whole year. This state of clinging is known as the "diapause."

When we enter our own darkness, we don't know where it will lead us and so it would make sense that part of our natural human journey is the diapause: it's our resistance to entering our darkness. What we discover though, just like the butterfly, is that when we bravely enter our darkness, lean into uncertainty and trust the process, we can then fly free.

HONOURING WHO I AM

The journey to embracing my gifts more fully really started when others reflected back what they saw in me. You really start to pay attention when you hear the same thing over and over from different people. In my experience, and through coaching others, it seems as if the journey to uncovering and embracing our gifts is often set in motion by others helping us see our gifts more clearly. We all seem to have that "gift blind spot" where our gifts come so naturally to us that we are too close to see them.

Part of honouring my gift was to focus it while also giving it room to grow. I shifted gears in my career; I left my corporate job and began coaching independently. I became certified as an Integral Coach, which gave me the tools and methods to further deepen my coaching practice. I now coach other people along their journey of belonging and becoming. This shift often sits at the challenging edges of the next growth or transformation in our life, from the present into the unknown, bravely stepping into our wobbly "what's next."

Over the past few years, the symbol of a lighthouse has been significant to me. It keeps coming up in spiritual readings, coaching metaphors, dreams, visions, and artwork, and in all the ways that synchronicities string themselves together.

During a spiritual reading, I was given this message: "You can do many things with your gift but it's up to you to decide. You've got to decide where your lighthouse goes. And once you put your lighthouse down, people will find you and you will help others with their gift by using your gift."

The lighthouse teaches us two important lessons. The first is that a lighthouse doesn't go running all around the island looking for boats to save. The lighthouse knows the only way she can help others is by staying rooted (in herself, her purpose, her intention). This is an important lesson for everyone but specifically for the highly sensitive/empath people who are helpers and healers. The second lesson the lighthouse teaches us is that some parts of our journey we travel alone in the darkness, weathering some big storms, but once we find our way through, we can bravely shine our light so that others may find their way too.

I am a beacon of hope, a bright light in the dark, a brave "way-shower" for those finding their way back home to themselves. I am a lighthouse.

Jane Middlehurst

Jane Middlehurst is a Certified Integral Coach® and transformational coach who supports leaders, coaches, creatives, and sensitives in expressing their unique calling in life and work. Often, this transformational work comes during a transition season in life, is guided by developmental growth within ourselves, and sits at the edge of our wobbly "what's next." It is the work of the brave who dare to lead a wholehearted life and, in many ways, leave the world a better place. Jane has spent more than fifteen years studying human development and designing custom leadership development programs and retreats for Canadian Fortune 500 companies. Her work has been deeply fulfilling and enriching; however, everything changed when she left an unhealthy corporate environment. During this transition season, she was reminded of how the Vikings would burn their boats on the shores of distant lands as a sign of "no going back"—they went all-in. In this way, Jane "burned the boats" on her former career and went all-in on the shores of her new coaching land. She bravely forged a new path by trusting her intuition to answer her deepest calling, and she now helps others do the same. Today, Jane guides and develops people in the power of their true being, bravely rising into leading their brightest vision. Jane offers one-on-one custom coaching programs as well as team and group programs.

@brave.rising

@janemiddlehurst

She Is

———— Hopeful

CHAPTER 18

MY BLESSING AND MY CURSE

Jackie VanderLinden

I grew up happy. Like, truly happy. My family wasn't perfect, but we were safe, and we were loved. I had parents who often danced in the kitchen on Saturday mornings while making breakfast. Life was good. I am the youngest of six children, and yes, as the baby of the family, I got teased by my older siblings, but they loved me too. My one sister, who is only a couple years older than I am, was my best friend (and my enemy on some days), but for the most part, our childhood was making mud pies in our playhouse or transforming my only brother's room into Barbie land. My family all went to church on Sundays, followed by a big family brunch. Even my older siblings who had married and moved out still all gathered together each week. I can still see the house full of family, food, and laughter; I remember my mother working away in the kitchen and then tucking us younger children into bed each night, saying our prayers together and kissing us goodnight.

My parents both worked full time in addition to running our hundred-acre farm. They didn't complain, and they showed me daily the value of hard work. Even with six children, my parents made Christmas and Easter mornings magical with beautiful gifts and surprises, and I always had a new, beautiful outfit for the first day of school. We worked hard every summer, together as a family in the fields. We spent afternoons at the river near our house, playing and swimming. I can fondly remember walking around our farm as a child, exploring and singing songs about nature. I was a happy child. I was also always the sensitive child.

I was still young, only about eleven or twelve, but I could feel things changing. Honestly, I don't remember exactly when or why it started, and there was no tragedy or trauma. I simply remember this growing uneasy feeling . . . that deep "sensitivity" kept grow-ing. I remember wanting to feel different—to not feel hurt by little comments. To not cry so easily. To be braver. I became bitter and tired of being the "baby" of the family. I wanted independence. I wanted time alone. Outside of me, my world was fine. But in my mind, something was wrong.

This sensitivity eventually became a darkness, almost a curse. It was a pain I couldn't understand. This darkness, now combined with teenage hormones, drove me deeper into a state of unease. And as a preteen and early teen in a small town in rural Ontario,

I did the only thing I felt I could do to stand out. I began to rebel.

My rebellion started with smoking a few cigarettes, then smoking some weed. In those moments it felt like an escape, but what I didn't see was that smoking weed was driving me deeper into my own darkness.

I began to self-harm, clawing at my own arms until they bled. I took pills. I wondered what it would be like to be free from it all, and yet I was scared enough to never go further.

This behaviour continued. My parents did their best to help their rebellious daughter. But truly, they didn't even see or even know most of it. At that time, it was fairly easy to hide my self-destruction.

During those days, I went on long walks. I sat by the river. Smoked. Wrote in my journal. Poured out all my painful thoughts onto paper. It felt right. It was one way of getting the pain out of my body—out of my head. I felt lost. I felt weak. I felt broken.

But that is the funny thing about life, about faith, and about trust. They will always show the way. Unfortunately, sometimes life needs to get worse before it gets better.

It was a regular summer day in early September. I was thirteen years old and just getting ready to head into high school. My parents, a few of my siblings, and I were working away in the field, looking to get as much done before the new school year started in just a few days. My mother, my siblings, and I were at one end of the field on the harvester and my father was at the other end on the tractor. We were working away when a man I didn't recognize walked up to my father. This seemed odd, but we kept working. Then suddenly I saw my father racing toward us on the tractor. Something was wrong. I could see it in his face as he approached. I don't even remember who said what, or any of the words that were spoken, but as we were all rushed out of the field I understood that my second-oldest sister, Jennifer, who was only twenty-seven at the time, had attempted to commit suicide.

We walked hurriedly. There were panicked conversations happening. Questions. Confusion. I remember reassuring my one sister as we walked together toward the house that Jennifer had only "attempted" suicide— they hadn't said that she was dead. In my mind, there was a clear difference. I knew the difference between thinking you want death and actually following through.

I don't remember walking into the house. I don't remember my mother picking up the phone or if the phone rang. All I can see in that moment is all of us standing in our kitchen, dirty from the field, still and silent, while my mother asked into the phone, "Is my baby alive?"

I witnessed my mother's heart break before my eyes. Her face instantly sank, and her body doubled over as she said, "No. No. No."

We rushed to the hospital and were ushered into a sterile hospital room. My brother-in-law sat beside my sister's lifeless body, holding her hand. We circled around her, held hands, and prayed.

I couldn't look at her face. I could barely mumble the words to the prayer. I just looked down and watched as my tears fell onto her arm.

This vision of her stillness with my tears on her arm still haunts me to this day whenever I hold hands to pray.

The next few days were a blur. Tears. Hushed conversations. So many people. Standing at the funeral home for hours as people shook my hand, hugged me, and shared their condolences. Then there were the words that my close family kept saying when they didn't think I could hear: "Keep an eye on Jackie . . . she's so much like Jennifer."

Remember, I'm the baby of the family. And Jenn was my second-oldest sister. She was fourteen years older than I was. She and my oldest sister were often like extra mothers to me. My whole family knew of my struggles, and their fear grew that Jenn's death would be my ultimate undoing.

But there's also one thing to realize about this time. It was 1995 and taking care of your mental health was not promoted like it is today. Suicide was not often talked about. At that time, at least to me, suicide felt like a dirty secret. It felt like it was our fault; that we had failed her. It was a topic that no one wanted to really acknowledge or discuss. When someone asked how she died, it usually put people into an awkward silence.

I was only thirteen years old. It was clear from my habits at the time that I did not know how to properly handle my emotions, let alone grief, which sent my unravelling even further. Before Jennifer's death, I didn't have a real reason for my pain. I didn't have a purpose for my pain. The loss of my sister allowed me to dive more deeply into my darkness. It felt right. I felt I deserved my space in the darkness. I had a reason to be angry and confused and to rebel.

Jennifer's funeral landed on my first day of high school. Just a few days earlier, I had been excited to get out of my small town's elementary school; I had been excited to meet new people, to do something different, to have more freedom. However, missing the first day of high school also meant facing questions on the second day. It was a painful and awkward way to start a new year at a new school. It felt like every new conversation I had went like this:

"Why weren't you here yesterday?"

"I was at a funeral."

"For who?"

"My sister."

"I'm so sorry. How did she die?"

My answer.

More awkwardness.

Of course, all my teachers were informed of my sister's death, which meant the inevitable looks of pity and the extra appointments with the guidance counsellor and the pastoral minister at the school to see "how I was doing."

How was I doing?

I was angry, scared, sad, and confused.

But my answer always came out as "fine."

My parents arranged for a grief counsellor to come to the house for a few weeks to talk to us as a family. I also attended a grief group for a while at school. It was helpful in some ways, but I didn't ever really feel comfortable there, and I never shared my own painful thoughts. I continued to rebel, to self-medicate, and to self-harm—anything to distract me from my reality.

The school year ticked by and days turned into weeks. Then one evening near the end of April, only seven months after my sister's death, I was in our family living room. It was already dark outside, and I was simply watching TV with my dad when the phone rang.

I don't remember the conversation, but after Dad got off the phone, he looked at me and told me that one of my close friends had been hit by a car while he was walking home. And it was bad.

This wasn't just any friend, though. It was a young man who, seven months earlier, had showed up to be a support right after my sister died. He didn't say much, but he showed up because he cared about me. He was a young man known to be full of life and beautiful energy who had, just days before, snuck to my house with a few other friends to hang out when my parents were away. He was a young man who, when he was over that night and I wasn't looking, read my journal—the journal that held some of the darkest thoughts after my sister's passing. He was a young man so full of life who wrote on the back of my journal, "If you are looking for death—stop, death will find you when death wants to" after reading about my pain.

Little did he know.

While sitting in that living room that evening, time escaped me. I remember my mother holding me, squeezing me tightly in her arms and saying, "You're too young to have to go through this." In that moment all I could think of was . . . then why am I?

I went to school the next day, wanting to see my friends and blindly hopeful. On my first break between classes, I found a pay phone at school and called to see how he was doing. "He didn't make it."

I felt numb as I floated down the hall. More tears. More confusion. More pain.

But I found that the days following were so different from those I experienced after my sister's death. First, I was surrounded by friends going through the same thing I was. After my sister's death, I felt alone and like people were avoiding me. Looking back, I don't blame my friends. Many did come to the funeral home when my sister died. Many of them reached out to give comfort. But it was limited and only for a few minutes. It seemed like everyone else in my family was surrounded by friends every step of the way. They gathered with us at our home and sat with us at the funeral home. But I didn't have someone there just for me, by my side. I was just there, feeling out of place—the baby sister, who is so much like Jennifer.

Sitting in the funeral home seven months later, I was surrounded with friends who, just like me, were ALL grieving. We were ALL there for each other. The grief was painful (in those first weeks it all felt unbearable), and yet, I didn't feel so alone. No one talked in hushed tones about a young boy who got hit by a car and died. In contrast, there were loud voices, and friends going to the city and to the newspaper to petition to have more lights installed on that dark street. There were flowers by the roadside as a reminder, and to honour. We shared this grief so openly.

When my sister committed suicide, no one rallied to support mental health awareness. It was such a different time in history and before everyone had cell phones and social media accounts to broadcast on. The "way" my sister died wasn't talked about often. It was "just" a tragic loss.

So, while I continued to deal with the confusion of this accumulating grief, my parents, in all their own pain, did their best to carry on and support me while I continued to rebel and spiral. Looking back, and as a mother now, I don't know how my parents were so strong in guiding me during this time, all the while living out their worst nightmare. I see now how fortunate I was to have had people like them—people who didn't give up on me during those days and who fought for me. Because truly, if they hadn't, I don't know where I would be today.

I had people who loved me even when I was ungrateful. I had people who believed in me even when I was broken and lost. And that's why I am here today. That's why I can write these words you are reading now. That's why I share this story—with the hope that other people will read it and not cast that kid aside. There were (and still are) many like me. Beautiful lost souls.

I wish I could say that this awareness and no longer feeling alone instantly helped things get better, but they didn't. Grief is a process, and I still struggled with my dark emotions, but slowly, over time, I began to open up. I began to see that I was surrounded by love and support. I began to understand my own strength. I began to see my emotions as a connection to the heart. I began to see my blessings. But I had to open up to the emotions and welcome in the healing.

I realize now, after years of self-discovery and self-development, that the darkness I felt wasn't really darkness at all. It was simply a deep unknown, and at that time, the unknown felt scary, yet intriguing. I now identify those feelings as a part of my spirituality—a longing, a knowing, a piece of my heart. I am a seeker, always looking deeper, not to dig for more problems but to come to an understanding and to find the light. Often now in my seeking, I can feel hope; I can feel a solution before I can even see it or understand it.

I am someone who clearly identifies as an empath. I feel EVERYTHING, and I feel it DEEPLY. Mentally, emotionally, physically. Good or Bad. And so, every day, this is my blessing and my curse.

This daily struggle has taught me, however, that I get to choose.

I get to choose to see these deep emotions as a blessing or as a curse. I can choose to use these deep emotions to dig a dark hole to crawl in, or I can choose to use it as a way to build myself and others up.

Everyone's journey is different. But many have been in that darkness with me—that darkness where there feels like there is no light, no space, no air, no hope; a space where physical pain seems like an obvious choice over the pain that is going on in your head and heart. But now, I see I had choices all along.

I now choose life daily. Sometimes, I choose moment by moment so as to not go to that dark space anymore. Don't get me wrong; I still find myself on that edge sometimes, in that struggle. I'm human. I struggle. I'm far from perfect. But I've also worked to surround myself with wonderful people and have armed myself with tools to support my body, mind, and heart daily.

And so, I write, just like I've always written. It's been one of my most powerful, cathartic tools along the way. I write to heal myself and to hopefully let others know that whether you are struggling in a dark space yourself or know someone who is—**don't give up.** Life isn't perfect. No one's life is perfect. But we are each here for a reason. And when the pain of it all feels like too much, know that sometimes we must break and fall apart so that we can put our lives back together in a different, more beautiful way.

Jackie VanderLinden

Jackie VanderLinden is a holistic coach, yoga teacher, and speaker who has nearly twenty years in the health and wellness industry. During those years, Jackie experienced many incredible, eye-opening moments in her own journey as well as witnessing the transformation of many of her clients, all of which has allowed her to pinpoint the key areas that tend to leave women feeling run down and defeated when it comes to taking care of their minds and bodies in a busy world.

Jackie is known to be full of heart and incredibly passionate about supporting women to get more out of their lives with less work. She truly believes that all women can be healthy and happy and live big, beautiful lives by simplifying a few key areas. She shares this knowledge and enthusiasm through her many speaking engagements, her classes, and her podcast called Less Is More.

Jackie is notorious for her endless energy, positivity, and resiliency. After overcoming incredible losses and numerous obstacles in her life, Jackie knew she could not just walk aimlessly through her days, so she left her previous 9:00-to-5:00 "life" to pursue her dreams and passions.

She now happily works remotely from her small hobby farm in southern Ontario, Canada, where she lives with her husband, daughter, dog, rabbits, ducks, and chickens. In her downtime, you will catch Jackie reading, working out, playing guitar, or simply hanging out with her family and friends.

🌐 www.holisticjackie.com

📷 @holisticjackie

f holisticjackie

To my parents who have shown me over and over throughout our lives their unconditional love for each other and their family as well as their strength and perseverance in the most challenging times. You two have been, and still are, guiding lights in my life. Thank you for believing in me and never giving up on me.

FINAL WORDS

As we conclude the second book in *The Great Canadian Woman: She Is Strong and Free* series, we are so incredibly proud of the womxn who shared their stories here.

The hope is that after reading this book, you feel inspired in knowing that our struggles do not define us and that we are capable of overcoming and rising stronger from any adversity. The hope is also that you see yourself in this book, perhaps not in the stories themselves but in the hearts of those who wrote these pages.

We are all Great Canadian Womxn. And as this series continues, we hope to share more empowering stories, more of Canada's beautiful diversity, and more truths.

Now, before you close this book, think of a Great Canadian Womxn who has influenced your life and tell her that. Then, entertain in your own mind that you, too, are that Great Canadian Womxn.

She Is Strong.

She Is Free.

She Is Courageous.

She Is Empowered.

She Is Kind.

She Is Loving.

She Is Bold.

She Is Fierce.

She Is Passionate.

She Is Smart.

She Is Brave.

She Is Curious.

She Is Hopeful.

She Is Inspiring.

She Is You.

COVER DESIGN: THE CREATIVE PROCESS

Creating the cover for *The Great Canadian Woman—She Is Strong and Free II* took some deep thought and required putting some feelers out into the community. I asked womxn what imagery the phrase "strong and free" brought up for them and what it meant to them to be a Canadian womxn. Each response embodied the wilderness, a connection to nature, the strength felt in the mountains, and the freedom witnessed in wolves howling at the moon or birds soaring the skies. I knew we needed something bold; an image that packed a punch and stood out from other covers in the industry. It needed to be something unique, something that represented both the brand that would carry the stories as well as the womxn who would be writing them. The upward triangle references The Great Canadian Woman branding logo but is also the symbol for fire—we are blazing trails for other womxn to share their stories, and the cover absolutely had to embody that fact. The mountains are those we climb, that inspire and ground us, and the ones we must move to accomplish our goals and overcome adversity in our day-to-day lives. Symbolizing the steadfastness that is required to endure the storms of life are the weathered pines; our roots grow deep so we can stand tall against all odds. As womxn, mothers, entrepreneurs, authors, and humans, we are ever changing, waning and waxing from our radiance and creative flow to the dark side that requires reflection, thought, and healing. Thus, the crescent moon. And because we are free and fierce in our ability to take flight, the eagle soars over everything without doubt that her wings will carry her far and wide.

Falon Malec

ENDNOTES

Janice Gladue

Brown, Brené. *The Call to Courage*. Directed by Sandra Restrepo. Netflix. April 19, 2019.

Rebekah Mersereau

Gough, Emily. Room to Grow. Podcast. Episode 207. "The Power of Storytelling and How to Share." https://emilygoughcoaching.com/biz-tips-the-power-of-storytelling-how-to-share/, retrieved November 5, 2020.

1. Brown, Brené. *Daring Greatly: How the Courage to be Vulnerable Transforms the Way We Live, Love, Parent, and Lead*. Gotham Books, 2012.

Steve Maraboli: https://www.goodreads.com/quotes/319476-plant-seeds-of-happiness-hope-success-and-love-it-will, retrieved October 28, 2020.

Lindsay Anderson

1. Caroline Myss: https://www.myss.com/archetypes-in-depth-the-prostitute/, retrieved October 21, 2020.

2. Campbell, Rebecca. *Light Is the New Black: A Guide to Answering Your Soul's Calling and Working Your Light*. Hay House, 2015.

Emily Murcar

Docter, Pete and Ronnie Del Carmen. dirs. *Inside Out*. Pixar Animations, 2015.

Ben Bennot: https://www.goodreads.com/quotes/6979688-how-we-walk-with-the-broken-speaks-louder-than-how, retrieved November 2, 2020.

Sarah Vaill-Ciano

1. Brené Brown: https://brenebrown.com/blog/2018/05/04/in-you-must-go-harnessing-the-force-by-owning-our-stories/, retrieved November 2, 2020.

Kimberly Davis

1. https://www.sciencedirect.com/topics/medicine-and-dentistry/hypnagogic-hallucination, retrieved November 4, 2020.

2. https://truehealthyfacts.com/lucid-dreams/, retrieved November 4, 2020.

Hafiz poem: https://symphonyforlove.blogspot.com/2014/10/inspirational-spiritual-poems-quotes-by.html, retrieved November 2, 2020.

Jane Middlehurst

1. Rumi: https://www.goodreads.com/quotes/103315-the-wound-is-the-place-where-the-light-enters-you, retrieved November 2, 2020.

Brooke Lillith: https://themindsjournal.com/the-healers-gift-is-her-own-wound/, retrieved October 28, 2020.

THE GREAT CANADIAN WOMXN

The Great Canadian Woman™ Inc. is an empowered multimedia organization and inclusive community that focuses on producing 100 percent Canadian content to put the spotlight on the powerful and inspiring womxn in Canada. What started as an idea for a podcast in 2018 to help Canadian womxn connect, learn, and grow has now become an empowered multimedia organization and inclusive community. In short, we put Canadian womxn in the spotlight because there is so much power, talent, heart, and expertise that goes unnoticed here. So, think of The Great Canadian Woman™ as a giant stage—for you. We help you get seen, heard, and noticed so you can make an impact with your story, insight, or expertise. Here, you have the opportunity to make an impact across Canada by becoming a published author in our coveted book series, broadcasting your message on our podcast, sharing your insights and experiences on our blog, and connecting with countless other Canadian womxn in our online community or at our events! We also provide an opportunity to learn about some of the tougher issues facing Canadians in our book club, so be sure to join us there, too!

> *"Gone are the days She remains humble and keeps her gifts, her wisdom, and her power to herself. Here, She owns her power. Here, SHE SPEAKS."*
>
> *- Sarah Swain,*
> *Founder and CEO of The Great Canadian Woman™ Inc.*

For more information on publishing, blogging, and podcasting opportunities, and information on events and merchandise, please visit: thegreatcanadianwoman.ca

⊙ @thegreatcanadianwoman 🅵 thegreatcanadianwoman

THE GREAT CANADIAN WOMAN— SHE IS STRONG AND FREE I

The Great Canadian Womxn is in all of us. She is the single mother who provides for her children, come hell or high water. She is the womxn who has a dream and musters up enough courage to go after it. She is the womxn who has quarrelled in the depths of pain and grief and finds her way back home to herself. She is the womxn who says "no" to what does not not serve her. She is the womxn who says, "enough is enough" and commits to a new way of living. She is the womxn who finds the strength to leave toxic relationships. She is the womxn who knows unconditional love. She is the womxn who takes the lead and lights the torch. She is the womxn who refuses to accept the limits that someone else placed before her. She is the womxn who knocks down doors and shatters glass ceilings. She is the womxn who finds a way out of no way, then turns around, extends her hand, and brings as many people as she can along with her. These stories grant us all the permission to live fully, love deeply, and fight like hell in the name of happiness.

Link to purchase publications: thegreatcanadianwoman.ca

THE GREAT CANADIAN WOMAN— SHE MEANS BUSINESS I

Normalizing hardship and adversity in business, career, and entrepreneurship by sharing how we got through the chaos, what we had to overcome, and how many times we had to stand back up behind the scenes, dust ourselves off, and keep climbing. The purpose of *The Great Canadian Woman—She Means Business* series is to encourage more Canadian womxn to keep their hearts locked into their professional dreams and to never, ever give up.

COMING SOON

THE GREAT CANADIAN WOMAN— SHE IS STRONG AND FREE III

Inspiring and empowering real-life stories from Canadian womxn who have navigated adversity in their life to give others hope of making it through to the other side of their own personal hardships.